Generation Gap

As expounded by the
Gnani Purush Dada Bhagwan

Originally Compiled in Gujarati by :
Dr. Niruben Amin

Publisher : **Mr. Ajit C. Patel**
Mahavideh Foundation
5, Mamatapark Society,
B/h. Navgujarat College,
Usmanpura, Ahmedabad-380014
Tel. : (079) 27540408, 27543979

© : All Rights Reserved - Dr. Niruben Amin
Trimandir, Simandhar City, Adalaj-382421,
Dist.:Gandhinagar, Gujarat, India

First Edition : 2000 copies, April 2000
Second Edition : 2000 copies, February 2003
Third Edition : 2000 copies, September 2004
Fourth Edition : 8000 copies, April 2005
Fifth Edition : 2000 copies, Nov. 2006
Sixth Edition : 5000 copies, January 2010

Price : Ultimate Humility &
"I Don't Know Anything"

Rs. 25.00

Printer : Mahavideh Foundation (Printing Division),
Basement, Parshwanath Chambers,
Nr. R.B.I., Usmanpura,
Ahmedabad-380014, Gujarat, India.
Tel. : (079) 27542964, 27540216

Printed in India

Trimantra
(The Three Mantras)
Namo Arihantanam
I bow to the Lord who has annihilated all the inner enemies of anger, pride, attachment and greed.
Namo Siddhanam
I bow to all the Lord who have attained final liberation.
Namo Aayariyanam
I bow to all the Self-realized masters who unfold the path of liberation.
Namo Uvazzayanam
I bow to the Self-realized teachers of the path of liberation.
Namo Loye Savva Saahunam
I bow to all who have attained the Self and are progressing in this path in the universe.
Eso Pancha Namukkaro
These five salutations.
Saava Paavappanasano
Destroy all the sins.
Mangalanam cha Saavesim
Of all that is auspicious mantras.
Padhamam Havai Mangalam
This is the highest.
ॐ Namo Bhagavate Vasudevaya
I bow to the One who has become the Supreme Lord from a human being.
ॐ Namah Shivaaya
I bow to all auspicious beings of this universe who are the instruments of salvation of the world.
Jai Sat Chit Anand
The Awareness Of The Eternal Is Bliss

❖❖❖❖❖

Note About This Translation

The Gnani Purush Ambalal M. Patel, also commonly known as Dadashri or Dada, had said that it would be impossible to translate his satsangs and the knowledge about the Science of Self-Realization verbatim into English because some of the meanings would be lost in the process. Therefore, in order to understand precisely the science of Akram Vignan and Self-Realization He stressed the importance of learning Gujarati.

Dadashri did however grant his blessings to translate his words into English and other languages so that spiritual seekers could benefit to a certain degree and later progress through their own efforts.

This is a humble attempt to present to the world, the essence of His Knowledge. This is not a literal translation but great care has been taken to preserve His original words and the essence of His message. For certain Gujarati words, several English words or even sentences are needed to convey the exact meaning; hence, many Gujarati words have been retained within the English text for better reading flow. At the first encounter, the Gujarati word will be italicized followed by an immediate explanation of its meaning in brackets. Thereafter the Gujarati word will be used in the text that follows. This serves as a two-fold benefit: firstly ease of translation and reading and secondly it will make the reader more familiar with the Gujarati words critical for a deeper understanding of this science. A glossary of all the Gujarati words is provided at the back of the book. For additional glossary, visit our website at :

www.dadabhagwan.org

Many people have worked diligently towards achieving this goal and we thank them all. Please note that any errors encountered in this translation are entirely those of the translators.

* * * * *

Introduction to The Gnani

One June evening, in 1958 at around six o'clock, Ambalal Muljibhai Patel, a family man, and a contractor by profession, was sitting on a bench on the busy platform number three at Surat's train station. Surat is a city in south Gujarat, a western state in India. What happened within the next forty-eight minutes was phenomenal. Spontaneous Self-Realization occurred within Ambalal M. Patel. During this event, his ego completely melted and from that moment onwards, he became completely detached from all of Ambalal's thoughts, speech, and actions. He became the Lord's living instrument for the salvation of humankind, through the path of knowledge. He called this Lord, 'Dada Bhagwan.' To everyone he met, he would say, "This Lord, Dada Bhagwan is fully manifested within me. He also resides within all living beings. The difference is that within me He is completely expressed and in you, he has yet to manifest."

Who are we? What is God? Who runs this world? What is karma? What is liberation? Etc. All the world's spiritual questions were answered during this event. Thus, nature offered absolute vision to the world through the medium of Shree Ambalal Muljibhai Patel.

Ambalal was born in Tarasali, a suburb of Baroda and was later raised in Bhadran, Gujarat. His wife's name was Hiraba. Although he was a contractor by profession, his life at home and his interactions with everyone around him were exemplary, even prior to his Self-Realization. After becoming Self-Realized and attaining the state of a Gnani, (The Awakened One, Jnani in Hindi), his body became a 'public charitable trust.'

Throughout his entire life, he lived by the principle that there should not be any commerce in religion, and in all commerce, there must be religion. He also never took money from anyone for his own use. He used the profits from his business to take his devotees for pilgrimages to various parts of India.

His words became the foundation for the new, direct, and step-less path to Self-Realization called Akram Vignan. Through his divine original scientific experiment (The Gnan Vidhi), he imparted this knowledge to others within two hours. Thousands have received his grace through this process and thousands continue to do so even now. 'Akram' means without steps; an elevator path or a shortcut, whereas 'Kram' means an orderly, step-by-step spiritual path. Akram is now recognized as a direct shortcut to the bliss of the Self.

Who is Dada Bhagwan?

When he explained to others who 'Dada Bhagwan' is, he would say :

"What you see here is not 'Dada Bhagwan'. What you see is 'A. M. Patel.' I am a Gnani Purush and 'He' that is manifested within me, is 'Dada Bhagwan'. He is the Lord within. He is within you and everyone else. He has not yet manifested within you, whereas within me he is fully manifested. I myself am not a Bhagwan. I too bow down to Dada Bhagwan within me."

Current link for attaining the knowledge of Self-Realization (Atma Gnan)

"I am personally going to impart siddhis (special spiritual powers) to a few people. After I leave, will there not be a need for them? People of future generations will need this path, will they not?"
~ **Dadashri**

Param Pujya Dadashri used to go from town to town, and country to country, to give satsang and impart the knowledge of the Self as well as knowledge of harmonious worldly interaction to all who came to see him. During his final days, in the fall of 1987, he gave his blessing to Dr. Niruben Amin and bestowed his special siddhis upon her, to continue his work. "You will have to become a mother to this whole world, Niruben" He told her as he blessed her. There was no doubt in Dadashri's mind that Niruben was destined to be just that. She had served him with utmost devotion day and night for over twenty years. Dadashri in turn had molded her and prepared her to take on this monumental task.

From the time of Pujya Dadashri's mortal departure on January 2 1988 to her own mortal departure on March 19th 2006, Pujya Niruma as she lovingly came to be called by thousands remained true to her promise to Dadashri to carry on his mission of the world's salvation. She became Dadashri's representative of Akram Vignan and became instrumental in spreading the knowledge of Akram Vignan throughout the world. She also became an exemplary of pure and unconditional love. Thousands of people from all walks of life and from all over the world have attained Self-Realization through her and are established in the experience of the pure Soul, while carrying out their worldly duties and obligations. They experience freedom here and now, while living their daily life.

The link of Akram Gnanis now continues with the current spiritual master Pujya Deepakbhai Desai whom Pujya Dadashri had also graced with special siddhis to continue to teach the world about Atma Gnan and Akram Vignan. He was further molded and trained by Pujya Niruma who blessed him to conduct Gnan Vidhi in 2003. Dadashri had said that Deepakbhai will become the decorum that will add splendor to the Lord's reign. Pujya Deepakbhai, in keeping with Dada's and Niruma's tradition travels extensively within India and abroad, giving satsangs and imparting the knowledge of the Self to all who come seeking.

Powerful words in scriptures help the seeker in increasing his desire for liberation. The knowledge of the Self is the final goal of all one's seeking. Without the knowledge of the Self there is no liberation. This knowledge of the Self (Atma Gnan) does not exist in books. It exists in the heart of a Gnani. Hence, the knowledge of the Self can only be acquired by meeting a Gnani. Through the scientific approach of Akram Vignan, even today one can attain Atma Gnan, but it can only occur by meeting a living Atma Gnani and receiving the Atma Gnan. Only a lit candle can light another candle.

✥✥✥✥✥

CONTENTS

PART ONE

The ideal role of parents towards children

1. Nurturing Values — 1
2. It is mandatory, so why complain? — 7
3. Do not fight in the presence of children — 9
4. Uncertified fathers and mothers — 11
5. Children improve with understanding — 17
6. Win them over with love — 21
7. Bad habits are overcome in this way — 24
8. A new generation with healthy minds — 29
9. Parental complaints — 32
10. Suffering due to suspicions — 47
11. How much inheritance for your children? — 49
12. Suffering life after life because of attachment — 52
13. Consider yourself blessed for not having children — 57
14. Relationships : are they relative or real? — 61
15. All relationships are merely give and take — 62

PART TWO

Children's Conduct Towards Parents

16. Dadashri's satsang with teenagers — 67
17. Selection of a wife — 70
18. Selection of a husband — 77
19. Happiness in life through service — 90

Important note: The pages referred to in brackets are references to the detailed satsang in the main full version of the book in Gujarati.

GENERATION GAP

THE RELATIONSHIP BETWEEN PARENTS AND CHILDREN

NURTURING VALUES

Questioner : Here, living in America we have money but we are lacking in moral values. What should we do when we have to live in such an environment?

Dadashri : Parents themselves should develop moral values that result in a loving family environment. The love from parents should be such that their children would not want to leave them. If you want to improve your child, the responsibility lies with you. You are bound by your duty to your child. (P.2)

Parents should instill the highest moral values in their children. Many parents in USA have complained to me about their children eating meat and indulging in other unacceptable activities. I asked the parents whether they themselves indulged in similar activities and they told me that they did. I told them that children would always imitate the moral values of their parents. And sometimes the children may behave differently outside of the home also. But your duty as parents should be to instill good values in them and you must not fail in this. (P.3)

You have to be careful and make sure that they do not eat non-vegetarian food. If you are eating non-vegetarian food, then after receiving this Gnan you should stop. (Gnan is the process by which Pujya Dadashri imparts to the aspirant the knowledge of the Self and separates the non-self from the Self). Children will follow your conduct. (P.4)

Questioner : When these children grow up, how are we to instill our religious values in them?

Dadashri : Children will learn whatever they see in you. So if you become religious, they will too. They learn from watching you. If you smoke, they will do the same. If you drink alcohol or eat meat, they will too. Whatever you do, they will imitate. They want to imitate and even go beyond their parents' deeds. (P.5)

Questioner : Will they not receive good moral values if we place them in a good school?

Dadashri : Children will only receive good values from their parents. They may receive some from their teachers; friends, peers and other people around them but the major part will come from the parents. Only when the parents are morally upright do their children also become morally upright. (P.7)

Questioner : If we send our children away to India for schooling, are we not forgoing our responsibilities?

Dadashri : No, you are not forgoing them. You can provide all the financial support needed. There are some excellent schools in India where even people of India send their children. These schools also provide good quality boarding and accommodation. (P.10)

Questioner : Dada, please give us your blessings so that we may lead a peaceful and a happy family life.

Dadashri : Your children will become good and virtuous by observing you. Children's behavior has degenerated through observing their parents' behavior. Parents behave inappropriately in the presence of their children. They often make suggestive gestures in front of them, so naturally the children become spoilt. What kind of impression will the children receive? There should be some restraint in your behavior. Just observe the effect fire has on a child. Even the child respects the boundaries of a fire.

Nowadays, the minds of parents have become fractured and restless and their speech has become careless and hurtful, which is why the children have become bad. Even a husband and wife use hurtful language towards each other. What is the role of a good parent? They should mould their child in such a way that by the age of fifteen, all the good moral values are instilled in them.

Questioner : Nowadays the moral standard is declining. That is where the problem lies.

Dadashri : No, it is not declining; it is practically gone. But now that you have met a Gnani Purush, the fundamental moral values and virtues of good human behavior will return in your life. Every young adult has the potential power to help the entire world. He just needs the right guidance and support. Without such guidance the youth has turned selfish and has a very self-centered view of life. They will prey on others for their own worldly comfort and happiness. He who renounces his own happiness can make others happy.

There was a wealthy businessman who was preoccupied with making money so I asked him, 'Seth you are so busy making money, do you realize that your household is in ruin? Your daughters and sons are running around and so is your wife. You have been robbed from all directions.' He then asked me, 'What should I do?' I told him, 'you have to understand and know how to live life. Don't make money your only pursuit in life. Take care of your health otherwise you will have a heart attack. Be attentive to your health, your money, to a moral upbringing of your daughters; you have to clean all the corners of your home. If you keep cleaning only one corner in the house, what about all the dirt and dust that collects in other corners? You have to clean all the corners.' How can you live life this way? So maintain good interaction with your children. Instill good moral values in them. If you have to suffer in the process it is fine, but give them good moral values. (P.17)

Questioner : We make every effort to improve them, but even then if they do not improve, should we as parents leave it to fate or destiny?

Dadashri : You make these efforts in your own way, but do you have a certificate to prove that your efforts are correct?

Questioner : Our efforts are based on our understanding and intellect.

Dadashri : I will give you an example of what your intellect is like: What kind of justice prevails when a person himself is the judge, the lawyer and the defendant? Your intellect will always be on your side, even if you are wrong.

Do not abandon them to fate, ever. Take care of them and keep an eye on them. If you abandon them, there will be no hope for them. Children bring with them their personalities at birth, but you have to help and nurture them so that they flourish.

Questioner : Yes we do all that but ultimately, should we just leave them to their fate?

Dadashri : No, you cannot leave them like that and if it comes to that then bring them to me and I will bless them and help them. You cannot just let go of them. It is too dangerous. (P.19)

A father was delighted when his child was tugging at his moustache. "Look! How cute! He is pulling my moustache!" he laughs. For goodness' sake, what is going to happen if you allow him to do as he pleases and you don't say anything to the child? All he has to do is give the child a little pinch so the child will come to realize that he is doing something wrong. The child should not be beaten; just a tiny pinch will suffice. (P.20)

One man calls out to his wife who is cooking in the kitchen. She calls back, 'What do you want? I am cooking!' He yells back "Come here, come quickly, come quick!' She comes running, "what is it?" she asks. 'Look! Look how clever our son has become', he points to their toddler. 'He stood up on his tiptoes and reached into my coat pocket and took out some money!' The toddler thinks to himself, 'this is the best thing I have done today. Now I know how to do this kind of work!' In essence, he has become a thief. So what happens next? It becomes instilled in the child's knowledge that to sneak money out of someone's pocket is an acceptable act. (P.21)

The fool! He should be ashamed of himself. What kind of a father is he? Does he even understand the kind of encouragement his child has received? In stealing, his child feels that he has accomplished something remarkable. Should the father at least not have some understanding of what to say in order to encourage or discourage his child? These are all uncertified fathers and untested mothers! If the father is a radish and the mother is a carrot, what are the children going to be like? Certainly not apples! (P. 22)

Parents of this era of the time cycle really do not have any skills or knowledge of how to raise children and often give them wrong encouragement. When they go out, the wife insists that the husband carry their toddler. If he refuses, she will nag at him, telling him he is also responsible for the child and that they both need to look after him. She keeps nagging him and he has no choice, so they end up carrying junior everywhere, all over the town. This kind of excessive attention suffocates the growing child. How can the child grow up to be normal? (P.23)

A bank manager once said to me, "Dadaji, I have never said a single word to my wife or my children, no matter what they say or do wrong, I do not say anything." He looked so self-assured, thinking that perhaps I would applaud him for his nobility. But instead I said, "Who on earth made you the manager of a bank. You do not even know how to manage your own family! You are the ultimate fool on this planet. You are useless!" He was shocked. Did he expect a medal for this? Your child does something wrong, you have to ask him, 'why did you do this? From now on don't do things like this' you have to scold him dramatically (in a make believe fashion) and convincingly; otherwise he will think that whatever he did was correct because his father condones it. Because he never said anything, his household was in ruins. You have to say everything, but dramatically, as if you are in a play on the stage of this world. He should play his role to its fullest, but without any attachment and abhorrence.

You should talk to your children every night and discuss things with them. Converse with them and explain things to them in an amicable manner. You need to pay attention to all the aspects of their development. They already have a good personality, but they need encouragement. You have to keep them in check and caution them. (P.24)

Teach your children good habits. Every morning after they bathe, teach them to pray for world peace and salvation. If you can do this, it would mean that you have succeeded in instilling good values in them. Pray with them, so they will learn from you. This is your duty as a parent. Everyday, you should also have them sing "Dada Bhagwan Na Aseem Jai Jai kar Ho" (Prayer to the Lord within). Many children have benefited from this and their concentration in their studies has improved. From a very young age, they will learn that God is within them. So many children have changed for the better that they no longer feel the need to seek other diversion. Going to movies is no longer their prime source of enjoyment. At first they raise objections, but after a while they remember how good it feels to say the prayers and they respond positively. (P.24)

IT IS MANDATORY, SO WHY COMPLAIN?

There is reward for good deeds a person does of his own volition (marajiyat), but people expect to be rewarded for their obligatory duties, which are mandatory (farajiyat). Parents expect appreciation from their children because they feel they have made a lot of sacrifices for them. Why are they looking for praise, when everything they have done and are doing is mandatory and obligatory?

A man was upset with his son because he had incurred a large debt from paying for his son's education. He kept complaining and reminding his son that he had taken out a loan to pay for his education and that if it hadn't been for him, his son would be nowhere. So I rebuked him and told him that he should not say such things and that whatever he did for his son was all mandatory. His son was wise but the man himself was lacking in commonsense and understanding. (P.30)

You should do everything for your children. But, some parents do not stop, even when their children tell them that they have done enough. Understand that it is a signal for you to stop when the children themselves tell you so.

A day will come when your son may want to start a business and you should help him. It would not be wise for you to get too involved in his business. He may even get a job, in which case he may not need your help. Then you should keep aside whatever money you had planned to give him. If he runs into any difficulties, you should give him some money. But, if you keep interfering with his life, it may aggravate him and force him to tell you to stay out of his business. Some fathers take this to mean that their son is not mature and that he does not know what he is saying. I tell the fathers they should consider themselves blessed for becoming free from this responsibility.

Questioner : What is the right thing to do? Should we still take care of our children or should we come to satsang for our own spiritual growth?

Dadashri : The children are already being taken care of, so what more can you do? Your goal now should be your own salvation. These children are already being cared for. Are you the one responsible for making them grow? Does the rosebush that you have planted also not grow in the night? Similarly the children too grow by themselves. You think the roses are yours, but the rose is its own entity. It belongs to no one. People act according to their own selfish motives and insecurities. Right now you are taking credit for everything you do and that is your ego.

Questioner : If we do not water the rosebush, it will wither away.

Dadashri : It will not come to that for sure. In fact your child will demand your attention if you do not give it to him. He may even throw tantrums. (P.39)

How is it possible to keep a balance between your duties

towards the worldly life and your spiritual progress? You should not neglect your duties. You are to fulfill your obligations, even if your son speaks to you rudely and is disrespectful towards you. What are your duties as a parent? Your duty as a parent should be to nurture and raise your child well and direct him on the right path. If he speaks to you in a disrespectful manner, and you do the same to him, he will become rebellious. Instead you should sit and explain things to him in a gentle and loving manner. There should be a spiritual understanding behind all your acts. If you do not allow spirituality to enter, something negative will enter in the vacuum. The vacuum will not remain for long. If a house is left vacant in these times, will squatters not trespass and occupy it? (P.39)

What is the role of a woman in the home? All the people in the neighborhood should be impressed by the way she fulfils her duties. The true religion of a woman is to raise her children with good moral values. And if her husband is lacking in these values, she should help him with that too. Religion is to make things better for one's family. Should one not try to make things better? (P.41)

Some parents get so involved and engrossed in their religious practices and rituals that they become irritated when their children disturb them. They become irritated with their children, within whom God resides, while they continue worshipping an idol of God. How can you ever become angry with your children? There is a living God present within them.
(P.41)

DO NOT FIGHT IN THE PRESENCE OF CHILDREN

If you are a vegetarian, you do not drink alcohol and you treat your wife with respect, your children will take note of your virtues. They will notice how other parents fight, whereas their parents do not. They learn this through simple observation.(P.47)

Everyday the husband fights with his wife in front of the children. As they observe this, they begin to think that their father is at fault. Your son may be small but he has a keen sense of justice. Girls on the other hand, will tend to side with their mothers because their intellect does not seek justice. Boys however, will judge their father because their intellect seeks justice. As the boy grows up, his judgment against his father will strengthen and his resolve to get even with him will also grow strong when he listens to others. Later in his life he will take his revenge on the father for abusing his mother. (P.48)

Parents should not fight in front of their children. They should set some standards for their conduct. If either parent makes a mistake, they should forgive each other. The children will witness this and be at peace. If parents want to fight, they should wait until they are alone, then they can fight as long as they want. When children witness their parents fighting they develop a negative attitude towards one parent or the other. So it is indeed the parents who are responsible for ruining their children these days. (P.49)

At the dinner table some fathers create a big fuss if there is too much salt in the food or something is not to his liking. They think that just because they are the heads of the household, they have the right to flare up any time. The children are terrified by such outbursts. They think that their father has gone mad, but they dare not utter a single word. So they suppress their emotions, but in their minds they form an opinion about their father. (P.51)

Children are tired of witnessing such scenes between their parents. Some even decide that they will not get married. When I ask them why, they tell me they have seen what marriage is all about when they witness their parents fighting and that they have come to the conclusion that there is no happiness in marriage. (P.53)

UNCERTIFIED FATHERS AND MOTHERS

A father once complained to me that his children had become defiant. I told him that their defiance was a reflection of his own past conduct. If he were a worthy father, his children would not retaliate. By making such complaints, he was exposing his own negativities. (P.57)

If you keep nagging your children and telling them off, they will become spoilt. Entrust them to me if you want them to be good. I will talk to them and mould them so that they will become good.

Disobedience in children reflects on parents. It is the parents who are at fault. So I have labeled them, "Unqualified fathers and unqualified mothers". It is no wonder the children turn out the way they do. That is why I tell you to learn the requirements of a certified parent before you marry. (P.59)

The father does not know the first thing about how to live life or how the world operates, so he keeps beating his children. Some fathers thrash their children as though they were dirty clothes. Children should be given the help to improve, not beaten. It is very wrong to beat children. I have seen people physically abuse their children as if they were punching bags. (P.62)

Real parents are those who manage to change their children's behavior through love and understanding, even when the child does dreadful things. But such love is not to be found, because the parents themselves are loveless. This world can only be won over through love. (P.63)

Questioner : Should we not be concerned at all about our children's upbringing and their moral values?

Dadashri: There is nothing wrong with showing concern.

Questioner: They can get their education from school, but what about development of their character?

Dadashri: Entrust the development of their character to the one who knows how to mold, the Gnani, the one who is adept in the art of molding human beings. You can mold your children the way you want to until they are fifteen years old. You cannot do anything after that. And when the son eventually get married, the task of molding becomes the wife's responsibility. Parents try to mold their children even when they are not skilled to do so and that is why they fail miserably and the results therefore, are far from agreeable. (P.64)

Questioner: What is the definition of a certified mother and father?

Dadashri: Uncertified parents are those whose children do not listen to them. Their own children have no love or affection for them and will be a constant source of aggravation to them. Can such parents not be labeled uncertified?

It is a sure sign that the parents have not fulfilled their duty to their children, when their children become disobedient. When the soil is bad and the seed is bad, the crop too will be bad. So how can parents boast that their children will be extraordinary like Lord Mahavir? How on earth can that be possible? What should the mother of Lord Mahavir be like? One can overlook it if the father is incompetent, but what should that mother be like? (P.70)

Many parents complain to their children that they do not listen to them. I tell the parents that it is because their speech does not appeal to their children. If the parent's speech pleased the children, then it would have an effect on them. The father keeps complaining that the child does not listen to him, when it is he who does not know what it takes to be a father.

You should speak in such a way, that children become interested in what you have to say. Only then would children listen to you. If you find what I say is appealing, then you will act on it.

Questioner : Your words have such a strong impact on our lives. That which could not be solved by our intellect and efforts, is solved by your words.

Dadashri : These are words that touch the heart. Words that touch the heart are inspirational, like motherly love. A certified father is he who can touch his children's hearts with his words.

Questioner : These children will not listen so easily and accept our words.

Dadashri : Would they listen to harsh authoritative words then? Such a tone in words does not help.

Questioner : They do listen, but only after a lot of explaining is done.

Dadashri : That is all right. It is quite normal. The reason why you have to explain to them is because you yourself do not understand. An understanding person needs to be explained only once. But do they understand when you do a lot of explaining?

Questioner : Yes.

Dadashri : That is the best way. You want to make them understand in whatever way you can. When you use force or authority, you are acting as though you are the only father in this world. (P.73)

How should a father behave towards his children? A father should never exercise the fear of power over his children or be overly strict.

Questioner : What if the children keep troubling him? Should he be lenient with them even then?

Dadashri : It is the father's fault that his children are troublesome. They only bother him because he is uncertified. The law of the world is that unless a father is unfit, the children would not bother him. (P.74)

Questioner : What if the son does not listen to his father?

Dadashri : The father should realize that the fault lies within him only, and leave it at that. If you knew how to be a good father, your child would listen to you, but you really have no idea about how to be a good father.

Questioner : Once a man becomes a father, will his children ever leave him alone?

Dadashri : How can that be? That would be impossible. Just look at how puppies scrutinize their parents for the rest of their lives. They watch their father going around barking while their mother is the one that does the biting.

The father is always the one who is blamed because he is always the one who is vocal. The children will always tend to side with their mother. So I warned a man that unless he treated his wife well, his children would take him to task when they are grown up. This has been the experience of many fathers. Children observe their father when they are young and helpless and as soon as they grow up, they will repay him, no matter what it entails. (P.74)

Questioner : Does that mean the fault lies entirely with the father?

Dadashri : Yes, the father alone. When a father is not worthy of fatherhood, even his own wife will oppose him. He will learn his lesson the hard way. She may remain silent for the sake of appearances, but for how long will she succumb to societal pressures of remaining married?

Questioner : Is it always the father who is wrong?

Dadashri : The father is always in the wrong. Because he does not know how to be a father, everything gets ruined. To be a father requires a lot of purity from within, so much so that even his own wife will respect and revere him. The standard of purity in relationships with his wife is this. His wife will beg to him for sex. Only when he attains this level, is he regarded as a certified father.

Questioner : If a father does not maintain his seniority in the family, if he does not assert his fatherly authority, is that not also a mistake on his part?

Dadashri : No it is not a mistake. Only then will things be resolved.

Questioner : If the father does not assert his authority, what guarantee is there that children will listen to him?

Dadashri : Of course there is. Your good character will have its effect and impact on the children and the world too.

Questioner : What can a father do if his children are of the worst possible kind?

Dadashri : There again, the root of the problem is the father. Why does the father have to suffer so? He suffers because of his own bad conduct from his previous life. If in past lives he had not lost control and not abused his children, he would not be suffering in this way now. Karmas were bound because he did not have the correct understanding, the original control. So here, I am emphasizing control, correct understanding. In order to practice control you must understand all its laws.

Your children are your mirror. They reflect your own faults.
(P.75)

If we had purity and good moral character, then even tigers would not harm us. So imagine what an impact it would have on our children. Our morality is displaced and that is why we suffer. Do you understand the value of morality?

Questioner : Would you please explain in detail what morality is, so that everyone can understand?

Dadashri : Morality is the deep inner intent (bhaav) never to hurt anybody even to the slightest extent, not even your enemy through the medium of thoughts, speech and acts. Shilvaan is one who is sincere, moral and does not harbor any intention to hurt any living being even to the slightest extent. Even a ferocious tiger will be pacified in the presence of such a person.

Questioner : From where would parents of today acquire such qualities?

Dadashri : Should they at least not strive to acquire some of these qualities? But instead because of the current era of this time cycle, people have become pleasure seeking, and self-gratifying. (P.76)

Questioner : What sort of a character should a father possess?

Dadashri : When children say that they would rather be with their father than be anyone else, it reflects on the father's character.

Questioner: Nowadays it is just the opposite. When the father is at home his children are out and vice-versa.

Dadashri: The character of the father should be such that his children would not like him to be away from him.

Questioner: So, what should a father do to become like that?

Dadashri: Once people meet me, whether they are children, elderly or even teenagers, they do not want to stay away from me.

Questioner: We all want to be just like you Dada!

Dadashri: You can, if you just observe me and act the way I do. If I ask for a Pepsi and if they say there is none, I settle for water instead. But you, on the other hand, become irate. Even if nothing is prepared for me by lunchtime, I will adjust and drink water instead, whereas you become demanding.

(P.76)

CHILDREN IMPROVE WITH UNDERSTANDING

Instead of nagging all the time, it is better to maintain your silence. Your attempts to improve your children by persistent nagging only makes them worse. Instead it would be better not to say anything at all. If they become spoilt, the responsibility is yours. Do you understand this? (P.84)

If we tell children not to do something, they will insist on doing it nevertheless and be worse off than before, so we will end up losing them altogether. These fathers have no clue about how to live their lives. They do not know the first thing about fatherhood and yet they become fathers. I have to explain everything to them using every possible means available. Those who have received this Gnan are able to raise their children well. They sit with their children and explain to them in a loving manner what the consequences of their mistakes will be. (P.87)

Generally when one parent rebukes the child, the other parent will stand up for him, so any hope of improving the child is ruined. The child will develop a fondness for the parent that takes his side and he will feel antagonism towards the parent who seeks to discipline. And when that child grows up, he will retaliate against that parent. (P.88)

In order to guide your older children, you must follow my Agnas (5 cardinal instructions given by the Gnani after the Gnan Vidhi). Unless children ask for your advice, do not say anything to them. You should tell them that it would be better if they did not ask you. If you start thinking negatively about them, you must immediately do pratikraman (apology coupled with remorse for any wrongdoing)

In this age, the power to improve others is lost so do not expect to improve anyone. Give up any hope of improving others. Unless there is unity within your mind, your speech, and your actions, your efforts will be futile. This means that you should speak whatever is on your mind and act accordingly. But this is not possible in this day and age. Interact reasonably with everyone in the family.

People do grave harm to themselves as well as to others in their efforts to improve them. First you must improve yourself, only then can you improve others. (P.93)

You should constantly maintain the intent that you want your child's understanding to improve. In doing so, you will notice a change after some time. Your child will eventually come to understand. You just have to keep praying for him. But if you keep nagging him, he will go against you. You have to adjust and accept things as they are. (P.96)

Generation Gap

If your complaint is about your child drinking alcohol, I would tell you to accept it because the fault is yours. I would however tell you to keep a positive intent for him. The law of nature and the law of the world are both different. People will always tell you that the child is at fault and you too will believe it, but nature's law says, 'the fault is yours.'

If you become a friend to your children, they will improve. But if you assert your authority as a parent, you will risk losing them. Your friendship should be such that the child will not go looking for comfort and guidance elsewhere. You should do everything a friend would do, with your child; play games, sports, drink tea together etc. Only then will he remain yours, otherwise you will end up losing him. Does any child accompany his father on the funeral pyre? These children are not really yours. Nature only makes them appear to be yours. First you should make the decision that you want to live with them as friends, and then you will be able to do so. If your friend is doing something wrong, how far will you go to caution him? You would only give him advice to the point where he listens, but you would not nag him. If he does not listen, then you would tell him that the decision is his. To be a friend to your child, you have to accept that from the worldly perspective you are his father, but in your mind you should think of yourself as being his son. When the father comes down to the level of his child, he will be accepted as a friend. There is no other way to become a friend.

Questioner : You have said that after our children turn sixteen we should become their friends. Why not become friends much earlier?

Dadashri : That would be very good, but you cannot be friends with them until they reach the age of ten or eleven. Until then, they may make mistakes and you will have to guide them and even discipline them if necessary. Those who have tried to exercise their authority as parents have failed miserably. (P.100)

Every parent should make an effort to better his child, but these efforts should be fruitful. Although you have become a father, are you willing to relinquish that authority in order to improve your child? Can you give up your belief that you are his father?

Questioner : If there is scope for improvement, all attempts to improve him must be made without any ego, a sense of 'doership' or abhorrence.

Dadashri : You have to let go of the sense and the feeling that you are his father.

Questioner : Am I to believe that he is not my son and I am not his father?

Dadashri : That would be the best thing. (P.101)

Some people greet me casually, while others heartily express their fondness and call me Dada. I have devised a way to reciprocate their feelings by balancing it out. When they address me as Dada, I would simultaneously in my mind, think of them as Dada, thus I would balance it out. Once I began to do this, I felt better. I felt lighter and people were more attracted towards me.

If I think of them as Dada, my words reach them and they feel delighted by the love and concern they receive from me. This is indeed a very subtle and important matter, which is worth understanding. You are fortunate to get this. If you can manage to do the same, it will be to your benefit. (P.103)

Questioner : The father wonders why his child does not adjust to him.

Generation Gap

Dadashri : That is because he continues to assert his authority as a father. This is wrong. The belief of fatherhood in itself is false. The belief that one is a husband is also wrong.

Questioner : Moreover, the father will assert his fatherhood by telling his children that he is their father and they should respect that fact.

Dadashri : I overheard a man yelling at his child, "Don't you know, I am your father?" What sort of a madman says such a thing? Does he even need to say that? The whole world knows this, so why does he need to repeat it?

Questioner : I have also heard children say to their parents, "Who told you to bring us into this world?"

Dadashri : How can parents hold up their heads when their children talk to them this way? (P.107)

WIN THEM OVER WITH LOVE

Questioner : When they make mistakes, should we not caution them?

Dadashri : All you have to ask them is whether or not they have thought about what they are doing and does it seem right to them. If they say no, then you can ask them why they continue to do so. They are capable of judgment and understanding. They instinctively know when they do something wrong. But when you start to criticize them, they will rebel and become indignant. (P.110)

Speak in such a way that the other person's ego does not arise. When you speak to your children, do not use an authoritative tone. When I speak to people, their ego is not stirred because my speech is free from ego that uses a commanding tone. (P.111)

Questioner : Is it demerit karma (paap) when we use harsh language at times while performing our duties?

Dadashri : What is the expression on your face when you use such language? Know that you have committed demerit karma when there is disgust in your expression and your face appears ugly. Always speak calmly and use gentle words. Never use bitter and ugly speech. Use your words sparingly and speak with love and affection so that one day you will win him over. Otherwise you will not succeed. Bitterness on your part will only serve to make him vindictive and harbor hatred towards you. He is helpless at the present time, but from within he is binding negative karmas to get even with you when he grows up. Love will work wonders for you although you may not see the results immediately. Just keep showering him with love and affection and later you will be rewarded with the fruits of this love.

Questioner : What should we do when despite trying to explain things to them, they still do not understand?

Dadashri : There is no need to make them understand at all. Just love them and make them understand gently. Do you ever speak harshly with your neighbors? (P.112)

How do we handle burning coals? Do we not use a pair of tongs? What would happen if we tried to hold the coals with our bare hands?

Questioner : We would get burned.

Dadashri : So a 'tong' is necessary.

Questioner : What kind of 'tong' should we use here?

Dadashri : There are people in your family that are like these tongs. They themselves do not feel hurt and they are also capable of handling someone who is hurting himself. When you talk to your child, you should have such a person present with you, who can reinforce whatever you say and help you deal with the matter. You will have to find a way to deal with the problem otherwise everyone will get hurt. (P.114)

If what you say does not make a difference, you should let it go. You are foolish to continue when you do not know how to explain things. Not only will it be in vain but you will also ruin your peace of mind and your spiritual progress as well. (P.116)

Questioner : Sometimes parents go overboard with their display of affection towards their children.

Dadashri : All that is being emotional. Even people who do not display their affection can be called emotional. Everything needs to be normal. By that I mean it should be dramatic. You have to play your part convincingly, just as you would in a play. Actors act out their roles so convincingly that even the audience believe it to be real. But when actors go off stage, they know that it was only a play and that it was not real. (P.118)

There is only one way to make this world better and that is through love. But what the world regards as love is merely attachment. All attachment by its very nature is associated with expectations. Besides, where is that love when your child breaks your expensive china? Instead you become irritated and angry; that is not true love. Children are looking for true love, but they do not find it. Only they understand their predicament. Not only can they not bear their plight, but they cannot express it either.

I have a way out for the young people of today. I know how to guide them. My love for them remains constant. My love does not increase or decrease. Love that fluctuates is not true love; it is attachment. Love that is constant is God's love. It wins everyone over. I for myself do not wish to win over anyone, but they surrender to my love. People have not yet seen true love. True love exists in the heart of a Gnani Purush. This love is absolute and unconditional. The Gnani's love is God's love. (P.119)

I get along very well with children. They make friends with me. As soon as I enter their homes, even the little toddlers would come and welcome me in. You pamper them, whereas I treat them with love. I do not pamper them.

Questioner : Dada can you explain the difference between pampering and loving our children?

Dadashri : After being away from his child for two years, a father is so overwhelmed that he hugs his child in a very tight embrace. The child feels smothered and bites his father's arm so that he would release him. Is this the way to show your love for your child?

Questioner : So what should a loving father do?

Dadashri : He should be gentle. He should simply pat the child gently or stroke his hair. This would make the child happy.
(P.121)

Never hit your child. Instead, gently run your hand over his head and explain things to him calmly. He will become good when you give him love. (P.123)

BAD HABITS ARE OVERCOME IN THIS WAY

Dadashri : Do you drink alcohol? Do you contaminate your body in this way?

Questioner : Yes, sometimes I do, when there is stress at home. I am being honest with you.

Generation Gap

Dadashri : Stop your drinking. You have become a slave to it. It is not right for you. This is Dada's agna, so you must not touch alcohol at all. Only then will your life run smoothly and you will no longer need to drink. If you read the Charan Vidhi (booklet given after the Gnan Vidhi); you will not need to drink at all. The Charan Vidhi will fill you with bliss. (P.126)

Questioner : How can I be free from addiction?

Dadashri : You must be convinced that the addiction is wrong and this belief will free you from it. Your conviction should not falter at all and your resolve to be free of the addiction should never change. Only then will you overcome it. But if you say that there is nothing wrong with your habit; then you will remain addicted and bound by it. (P.127)

Questioner : They say that if a person has been drinking and using drugs for a long time, it will affect his mind and the effects will last for a long time afterwards. How can one become free from such chronic effects?

Dadashri : These remaining effects are the reactions from the addiction. All the sub-atomic particles within the body (parmanoos) need to be cleansed. Once the drinking stops, what should he do then? He needs to keep repeating to himself that it is wrong to drink. He should never say that drinking alcohol is good. He must be absolutely convinced that drinking alcohol is wrong and that it is harmful. In this way he will be free from his addiction. If he ever supports the drinking by thinking or saying that there is no harm in it, he will suffer a relapse.

Questioner : What damage does alcohol cause to the brain?

Dadashri : Alcohol makes you lose awareness. When you

drink alcohol your awareness is shrouded by veils of ignorance. These veils of ignorance will accumulate and never leave. You may believe that they have dispersed, but they instead become denser and will turn you into a dull and ineffective individual. You will not be able to think positively or clearly. Those who have managed to overcome their addiction to alcohol have developed a positive attitude and thinking.

Questioner : Once alcohol has created this veil over the awareness, how can it be removed?

Dadashri : There is no solution for that. Time is the only remedy. The longer a person abstains from drinking alcohol, the clearer his thinking will be as the veils of ignorance disperse. He will begin to notice the difference as time goes by, but not immediately.

Understand that pleasure derived from eating meat and consuming alcohol will have to be repaid. The repayment for this will be that in his next life, he will have to take birth in a lower life form, in the plant or the animal kingdom. Every form of external happiness one enjoys will have to be repaid, so one must understand the gravity of this obligation. The world is not haphazard; it will demand a repayment. Only the experience of one's inner bliss does not need to be repaid. So remember you will have to pay back whatever you borrow.

Questioner : A person will have to repay as an animal in his next life, but what are the consequences of eating meat and drinking alcohol in this life?

Dadashri : In this life his ignorance will increase. As a result he will become callous and beastly. People around him will not give him any respect. (P.127)

There is no difference between eating an egg and eating a baby. Does eating someone's baby appeal to you? (P.129)

Questioner : Dada so many children have turned vegetarian because of you. Some however believe that eggs are a part of a vegetarian diet.

Dadashri : No. It is a wrong belief. They believe that eggs are without life(nirjiva), but one cannot eat anything that is non-living.

Questioner : This is a different perspective.

Dadashri : Different, but exact. Scientists have discovered that non-living things are inedible. Things are only edible if they contain life. The egg has a potential for life, but people have misconstrued this and taken advantage of it. One should never eat eggs. When children eat eggs, elements of passion and restlessness are introduced into their body, which will then lead to loss of control and discrimination. Pure vegetarian food is good for you even when eaten raw. Doctors may tell you to include meat in your diet, but they cannot be blamed because they act according to their understanding and intellect. But you are responsible for your own spiritual development. We have to look after our own spiritual development (P.130)

One parent complained to me about his children eating meat, I asked him whether he ate meat, he said he did sometimes and he would also occasionally drink alcohol. I told him that his children would stop when he stops. What do you expect from the children when they see their own father doing it? They think it is good for them to eat meat and drink alcohol since their father does it.

I asked the children if they get upset when they cut vegetables or fruits and they said they did not. Then I asked them if they would be able to cut a goat or a chicken and they categorically replied that they would not able to do so.

So you can only eat things that you can cut without hesitation. You must not eat things your heart will not accept, otherwise the effects will be detrimental and the resultant (indivisible sub-atomic particles) parmanoos will have an adverse effect on the heart. The children accepted and understood this and became vegetarians. (P.131)

Someone once asked George Bernard Shaw the playwright, why he did not eat meat and he replied: "My body is not a graveyard! It is not a cemetery for chickens. I want to be a civilized man." (P.132)

Questioner : Is it all right to feed magas (a heavy and rich sweetmeat made with a lot of ghee and sugar) to the children?

Dadashri : No, you should not feed magas to children. Magas or any such heavily fat-laden sweets cannot be given to children. Children's diets should be kept simple. Even their milk intake should be limited. People keep stuffing their children with dairy products. Such foods promote passion and excitement in children. Even at the age of twelve, a child will begin to have sexual thoughts. You should give your child the kind of diet that will decrease such hyperactivity. Children have no idea about all this. (P.132)

Questioner : If we suspect that our child is stealing, should we allow him to continue because we do not want to say anything?

Dadashri : You should express your disapproval on the outside, but from within, you should maintain equanimity and remain undisturbed. You should not be ruthless towards him if he steals. If you lose equanimity, you will become merciless. The entire world becomes merciless. (P.135)

You should tell your child to do pratikraman. He must be taught to apologize and repent for his actions and he should tell you how many pratikramans he does. This is the only way he is likely to improve. Make your child promise that he will not steal again. Keep explaining to your child from time to time so that he can come to understand. In his next life he will not steal because in this life he has accepted that it is wrong to steal. The act of stealing in this life is an effect from his previous life, which will come to an end, and no new accounts will be created because of his present understanding. (P.136)

This young boy confesses all his mistakes to me. He even admits to stealing. People only confess to someone with extraordinary qualities and nobility. Tremendous changes will take place in India through this process of pratikraman.

A NEW GENERATION WITH HEALTHY MINDS

Dadashri : Every Sunday a satsang is held near your home. Why do you not attend it?

Questioner : Every Sunday we watch TV, Dada.

Dadashri : What connection do you have with your TV? Even though your eyesight is bad and you have glasses, you still watch TV? In our country there is no need for TV or the theatre, because all the drama takes place right here in the streets anyway!

Questioner : Will we not stop watching television when our time to enter spirituality comes?

Dadashri : Lord Krishna has said this very thing in the Gita; that humans waste time unnecessarily. It is not considered a waste of time if one has to work for a living. But until you attain the true knowledge, this false knowledge will not leave you.

Why do people smear their bodies with 'foul smelling mud'

You should tell your child to do pratikraman. He must be taught to apologize and repent for his actions and he should tell you how many pratikramans he does. This is the only way he is likely to improve. Make your child promise that he will not steal again. Keep explaining to your child from time to time so that he can come to understand. In his next life he will not steal because in this life he has accepted that it is wrong to steal. The act of stealing in this life is an effect from his previous life, which will come to an end, and no new accounts will be created because of his present understanding. (P.136)

This young boy confesses all his mistakes to me. He even admits to stealing. People only confess to someone with extraordinary qualities and nobility. Tremendous changes will take place in India through this process of pratikraman.

A NEW GENERATION WITH HEALTHY MINDS

Dadashri : Every Sunday a satsang is held near your home. Why do you not attend it?

Questioner : Every Sunday we watch TV, Dada.

Dadashri : What connection do you have with your TV? Even though your eyesight is bad and you have glasses, you still watch TV? In our country there is no need for TV or the theatre, because all the drama takes place right here in the streets anyway!

Questioner : Will we not stop watching television when our time to enter spirituality comes?

Dadashri : Lord Krishna has said this very thing in the Gita; that humans waste time unnecessarily. It is not considered a waste of time if one has to work for a living. But until you attain the true knowledge, this false knowledge will not leave you.

Why do people smear their bodies with 'foul smelling mud' of these cinemas? It is to give them relief from their burning pain. The television and cinema are nothing but 'foul smelling mud'. Nothing of value can be achieved from it. I do not have any objections with the television. You are free to watch anything, but if your favorite show were going on at the same time as a satsang, which would you prefer? If you had to take an examination at the same time as a luncheon invitation, what would you do? That is how you should look at the situation.

Questioner : Children do not get enough sleep because they watch TV late in the night.

Dadashri : You are the one who bought it for them so why would they not watch it? You have allowed them to become spoilt. You added a problem where there was none. (P.142)

This young boy ogles at his reflection in the mirror and goes on admiring himself in his new pants. Who is he trying to impress? No one has the time to look at him; people are preoccupied with their own problems and worries. (P.144)

If you were to ask every generation whether their elders constantly nagged them, they would say that they did. The cycle repeats itself. Children are not ready to accept our old fashioned ways of thinking and that is why we have problems. I tell parents to become modern in their thoughts. How is it possible? It is not easy to become modern. (P.149)

Nowadays the generation is broad-minded. It is not like the narrow-minded, petty and superstitious generations that preceded it. In previous ages, Brahmins did not mingle with people of an inferior caste. They treated other castes with contempt. In comparison, this generation is open and receptive and healthy-minded.

Keep positive intents (bhaavs) for your children. This will bring good results. They will change for the better and this will happen naturally. Today's generation is the best that has ever been.

Why do I say this? What special qualities do they possess? They are not bigoted like the contemptuous so-called superior caste egoists of olden days. Their only weakness is their fascination for the material world, whereas children of previous generations had lot of prejudice against other children of lower castes.

Questioner : Nothing like that exists nowadays.

Dadashri : They come with clean accounts from previous life. They have no greed and care little about false pride and validation. Until now, people have been full of pride, greed and anger, but these poor beings are just obsessed with material things.

Questioner : You say that this generation of youth is healthy-minded, but on the other hand they have some form of substance addiction and other associated problems.

Dadashri : They may seem addicted, but only because they do not find a right path for themselves. It is no fault of theirs. They do have healthy minds.

Questioner : What do you mean by a healthy mind?

Dadashri : Healthy minds are those who care very little for possession. When we were young we would immediately pounce on things we thought we could keep. If we went out for dinner at someone's house, we would eat more than we would at our own home. From young to old, everyone was possessive in nature. (P.156)

What sort of people are you? In the past, Indian couples

never occupied the same bedroom. They always slept in separate rooms. Just look at the parents of today. They furnish their room with a double bed and so the children come to perceive this as being a natural thing. (P.158)

PARENTAL COMPLAINTS

A man complained to me about his nephew who would always wake up late every morning. This habit of his was very disruptive for everyone else in the household. He wanted me to reprimand his nephew. I told him that I would not do that, but I would make him understand. I spoke with the nephew and told him to pray for the strength to wake up early and I blessed him. I told the rest of the family members to be kind to him and to offer him an extra blanket if he needed it. I told them not to make fun of him. Within six months of this conversation, they began to see positive changes in him. (P.169)

Questioner : Today's children seem to be more interested in playing, than their schoolwork. How can we guide them towards education without creating any conflict?

Dadashri : Start a reward system. Tell them you will give them so much for getting good grades at school and passing all their exams. Give them some incentive. If they see immediate positive reinforcement they will seize the opportunity. Another approach is to love them unconditionally. If you give them love they will do what you tell them. Children readily listen to me and will do whatever I tell them. We should always try our best to give them the right understanding. We should never give up on them. We should make all the efforts. After that whatever they do is correct and you should accept that it was meant to be. (P.171)

Questioner : My main question was how we should get them to understand the importance of education. They still do not

Therefore, you must learn how to deal with them. (P.177)

Questioner : When our grown up sons are fighting amongst themselves and we realize they will not come to any understanding, what should we do?

Dadashri : Have a talk with them and tell them it is not worth fighting. Such internal fights will result in financial ruin.

Questioner : And if they are still not ready to listen, then what?

Dadashri : Let it be. Let it be.

Questioner : When they fight amongst themselves, things get out of control and we wonder how the problem becomes greater.

Dadashri : Let them learn their lesson. By fighting amongst themselves they will eventually come to their senses. They will not be receptive if you keep preaching to them. This world is meant to be observed. (P.177)

In reality, they are nobody's children. It is because of your past accounts that you have been burdened with them, so you should try your best to help them, but remain detached from within. (P.178)

Who is the first to complain? In Kaliyug, the current era of the time cycle there is no unity of thoughts, speech and conduct, and so it is always the guilty one who complains first. In Satyug, the past era of the time cycle when there was unity of thoughts, speech and conduct, it was always the innocent person who complained first. In this era, people who dispense justice will always favor the one who comes forward first and is the first to speak. (P.178)

There are four children in a family. The father keeps getting annoyed with the two that do nothing wrong and never says anything to the two that keep making mistakes. All this stems from the root cause of their past lives. All children should be treated equally. If you favor one over the others, everything will be ruined. Are you still partial towards one? (P.179)

Questioner : My son frequently gets upset very easily and sulks.

Dadashri : It is because people give too much importance to the boys and not enough to the girls. The girls are less likely to sulk. (In India, the male child receives more importance.)

Questioner : Why do they sulk, Dada?

Dadashri : It is because you constantly give in to them. Just let them come to me and sulk! They do not sulk with me because I never give in to them. Even when they refuse to eat, I would not bother with them, whereas you make a big fuss and insist that they eat. I do not coddle them to eat. In doing so you are reinforcing bad habits. I know what bad habits it creates. When he gets hungry, he will eat, you will not have to pamper him. I know of other tactics. And sometimes if he is being very obstinate, he may not eat anything even if he is hungry. So then I would communicate directly with his Soul. You should not do this; you should just continue to do whatever you normally do. Children do not sulk with me. What good does sulking do?

Questioner : Dada, show us your tactics, because the sulking and pampering goes on day in day out. So if you give us your key, it will help us all.

Dadashri : They sulk because of your own selfish interest and expectations. Why should you have so many selfish motives?

Questioner : I don't understand what you mean by selfishness. Whose selfishness?

Dadashri : A person who is sulking does so because he knows that you want something from him.

Questioner : Should we keep our selfish expectations hidden?

Dadashri : There should not be any such motives. Why should you have any expectations? You will get whatever your karma has in store for you. If you harbor any expectations from him, he will become even more obstinate and difficult. He will continue sulking. (P. 179)

Questioner : How can we pacify a youngster who throws temper tantrums?

Dadashri : How will it help the situation by getting rid of his temper?

Questioner : He will not fight with us.

Dadashri : As a parent, you should conduct yourself in such a way that he does not detect anger in you. When he sees you get angry, he will decide that he can be angrier than his father. If you stop getting angry, he will too. Look at me. Since I have conquered my anger, no one fights with me. Even when I tell them to get angry with me, they shrug their shoulders. (P. 181)

Questioner : We have to get angry with our children so that they do the right thing. Don't we have to fulfill this duty as parents?

Dadashri : Why must you become angry? What is wrong with simply explaining things to them? You are not creating anger.

Anger just happens. The anger that you display is not considered anger. It is not considered anger to scold your child. So show anger. It is acceptable to demonstrate anger, but instead you become angry from within. It is one thing to display anger and another to become angry. (P.181)

Questioner : What is the reason behind anger?

Dadashri : Weakness. Anger is a weakness. It is this weakness that makes a person angry. He himself does not get angry. After he gets angry, he realizes that it was wrong. He is remorseful, which goes to show that it is not in his control. This machine, this body and its contents, gets overheated, so you should wait for it to cool down and then you can pursue the matter.

(P.182)

When you become irritated with your children, you are binding new karma for your next life. There is nothing wrong in displaying irritation towards them as long as you do not feel and suffer the irritation. It should be dramatic.

Questioner : They do not become quiet unless we scold them.

Dadashri : There is nothing wrong in scolding them. But when you become involved in the scolding your facial expression changes to one of disgust. In doing so, you will bind negative karma. Go ahead and scold them, but keep your facial expression pleasant. It is because your ego arises that your facial expression becomes ugly.

Questioner : Then children will think that we are not serious when we scold them.

Dadashri : It is enough even if they think that. Only then will it have an impact, otherwise it will not affect them at all. If you keep scolding them, they will conclude that you are a weak person. They even tell me that their father is such a weakling because he keeps scolding them. (P.183)

Questioner : We should not scold them to the point where it begins to have a negative effect on our own minds.

Dadashri : Scolding with such intensity is wrong. You should scold them in a make-believe manner, as though you are acting out a role in a play. In a play, a person will say anything but he knows from within that it is not real. (P.186)

Questioner : What should we do when scolding is necessary but it hurts them?

Dadashri : You should then ask for forgiveness from within. If you have over-reacted in anger towards someone, go directly to that person and apologize. And if that is not possible, then you must do pratikraman from within. Ask for forgiveness from his Soul. You yourself are pure Soul(Shuddhatma), and you have to tell 'Chandulal', your relative self, to do pratikraman. You have to keep the two separate. Tell yourself from within that you should speak in a way that does not hurt anyone. And despite this, if it still hurts your children, you have to tell 'Chandulal' to do pratikraman.

Questioner : How are we to ask forgiveness if the child is very young?

Dadashri : You should ask for forgiveness sincerely from within. With 'Dada Bhagwan', your pure Soul as your witness, you should first confess your wrongdoing (alochana), apologise for it (pratikraman) and resolve never to repeat the mistake (pratyakhyan) to the Soul within the child. This will immediately reach his Soul. (P.186)

Questioner : If we scold our children for their own sake, are we committing a sin (paap)?

Dadashri : No, you are actually binding merit karma (punya). If you scold your child, or even beat your child for his own good, you bind punya. That anger binds punya, because it is for the welfare of the child. If it were a sin to do so, then none of these religious teachers and ascetics would attain liberation. A guru that continually reproaches his disciples binds merit karma, because his intentions are good and he has their best interest at heart. According to the Lord there is no injustice. It is only sinful when one becomes angry for selfish gains. How beautiful and precise is nature's justice! This justice is the foundation for one's ideal duties and obligations.

When you scold or beat your child for his own benefit, you bind merit karma, but when you do it with a belief that you are his father and that he needs beating and you assume the role of a father, then you will bind demerit karma (paap).

Questioner : The father may get annoyed but what if the son also gets annoyed in response?

Dadashri : Then the son binds demerit karma. In the kramic path, the traditional spiritual path, if the Gnani Purush were to become annoyed with his disciple, he would bind the greatest of merit karma. This merit karma is called punyanubandhi punya (good karma which leads to greater good karma). His annoyance is not in vain. These are not his children, he has nothing to do with them and yet he is concerned about their welfare and so he scolds them.

Here we do not reprimand anyone at all. When children are reprimanded, they will not tell the truth and they will learn to hide things. This is how deception arises in the world. There is no need to reprimand anyone in this world. If your son comes home from watching a movie and you tell him off, the next time he wants to go to a movie, he will make up an alibi. If a mother is too strict, her children will not know how to interact with others. (P.188)

Questioner : I scold my children when they eat too many chocolates and drink a lot of Pepsi.

Dadashri : Why do you need to scold them? Just explain to them how unhealthy it is for them to eat too many chocolates and drink too much Pepsi. Does anyone scold you?

This is false assertion of your ego as a mother. You do not know how to be a good mother and yet you keep yelling at them unnecessarily. You would realize this if your own mother-in-law were to scold you. The children will feel that their mother is worse than a mother-in-law. So stop scolding your children. You can talk to them gently and explain to them that they will ruin their health if they eat the way they do. (P.191)

If your child is doing something wrong, you do not have to keep on at him all the time. What happens if you do? I once saw someone thrashing his child as though he were a washing rag. What kind of a father puts his child through such abuse? Does he have any idea what the child is thinking from within? He cannot tolerate such abuse so he vows to himself that he will get even with the father when he grows up. And then he treats his father in exactly the same way when he is older. (P.196)

No one in the world improves through physical or verbal abuse. They benefit from being shown the right way to act. (P.199)

There was a man who would come home late every night. What he did outside the home is not suitable to mention. The rest of the family was at a loss as to whether to reprimand him or throw him out of the house. When his older brother tried to talk to him, he threatened to kill him. His family came to me for advice. I told them not to say anything to him or else he would react adversely. And if they were to throw him out of the house, he would turn into a criminal. I told them to let him come and go as he pleased without judging him. They were not to harbor any attachment (raag) or abhorrence(dwesh) towards him. They were to maintain equanimity and compassion towards him. After three or four years, this man turned into a good person. Today he is an invaluable asset in the family business. This world is not useless, but we need to know how to extract use from it. All beings are divine and each person has his or her own duty to fulfill. So do not harbor any dislike for anyone. (P.200)

I witnessed a man kicking the door of a toilet and I asked him why he was doing so. He told me that although he kept cleaning the toilet, it still smelt bad. How foolish it is to keep kicking the door because the lavatory smells bad? Whose fault is it?
(P.201)

So many parents keep beating their children. Are these children punching bags? They are as fragile as glassware. So you must handle them with care. What would happen if you throw glassware? You must handle the children gently. (P. 204)

You worry about the children you have now, but what became of the children you had in your past life? What did you do with them? You have left your children behind in each lifetime. In some previous lives, you have even abandoned them while they were still helpless infants. Even though you did not want to, you were torn away from them. You have forgotten all that and then in this life you have some more children. So then why are you quarelling all the time with your children? Guide them towards spirituality and they will improve. (P.209)

There was a little boy who was very difficult and he refused to swallow some cough syrup that his mother was giving him. He resisted his mother as she held out the spoon, so she pinched his nostrils and shoved the syrup into his mouth so that it gurgled down his throat. The next time she ventured do this he spit the medicine in her face! This is the quality of a child; nine months in the mother's womb without paying rent and this is how she is repaid! (P.221)

A man complained to me that while two of his three sons were brilliant and hardworking, one of them was a failure. He admitted that he had no complaints about two of his sons but the third one would come home drunk every night and was a constant source of misery for him. If the son saw that his father was still awake, he would yell abuse at him, so the father would spy on his son from behind a window. As soon as the son came home he would collapse on his bed and doze off to sleep, while his father would lay awake half the night worrying about him. I told the father that the fault was his own because he was the one was suffering. I went on to tell the father that he was responsible for his son's drinking problem and that in his past life he pushed this addiction onto his son and then abandoned him. So now in this life he was paying for this debt that he created in his past life. Now he will have to endure it. The fault is of the sufferer! While the son doses off to sleep soundly; the father lies awake all night tormented by worries. (P. 222)

A daughter-in-law thinking that her father-in-law is in another room and cannot hear her, tells her friend, 'My father-in-law is not very intelligent'. Now he just happens to overhear her comment and it becomes a source of ailment for him. How should he tackle this situation? He should just consider that had he been elsewhere in the house, he would not have heard her and her comment would not cause him to become sick, and therefore this was a sickness of error. So all he has to do is break the error. All he has to do is to assume that he was sitting further away and that he did no hear anything. This way the mistake is destroyed.

People used to gossip even about Lord Mahavir. People can say whatever they want, but you should destroy your mistakes. People will say whatever they please, but know that it is only because of your own karma that they are able to speak this way about you. (P. 223)

Once the ego becomes established in a child, you can no longer say anything to him. He will learn from his own mistakes. You can only discipline children until they are five years old. And between the ages of five to sixteen years, you may occasionally have to scold them. But when they reach the age of twenty, you cannot say anything to them. You cannot utter even a single word of admonishment. It is a mistake to do so. If you do, he may even shoot you. (P.225)

I am saying that one should not give advice unless it is asked for. If someone asks you, then you should give him advice according to what you think is right, but you should also tell him that he is free to do whatever he deems right for him and that you are merely making a suggestion In this way you will do what you have to, without hurting his feelings. Say whatever you need to tell him, but do so with humility and respect for him.

In this day and age, it is better to speak sparingly. In this day and age people's speech is harsh and abrasive. The words hurt like rocks and so it is better to speak as little as possible. It is not worth saying anything to anyone; in fact we make things worse. People will always act contrary to what they are told. Everything will run smoothly even in your absence. All this is nothing but your ego. The day you stop arguing and nagging your children, they will begin to improve. It is because your words do not come out right that they get aggravated. They do not embrace your words, but simply throw them back at you. You have to fulfill your duties as a parent and provide for them, but you cannot say anything to them. There is no benefit in you telling them anything. Are you able to come to this conclusion? Now they are all grown up, it is not as if they are going to fall down the stairs. Why are you compromising your spiritual progress? It is not worth expending all your efforts on your children. Instead of fighting with your children, the results would be better if you were to remain silent. By fighting, your peace of mind as well as your children's will be lost. (P.226)

The children call you bad names and you call them bad names. This creates an atmosphere of hostility, which can flare up at any time. So you just have to change your opinion by telling yourself, 'after all he is a good person'. (P.228)

Questioner : How should we behave with children when there is a conflict?

Dadashri : You should not feel any attachment or abhorrence towards them. If they damage or spoil things, you should not have negative feelings towards them. See them as pure Souls. Your troubles will end if you do not have any attachment or abhorrence towards them. And this Gnan is such that you will not have any attachment or abhorrence (P.228)

If your mind becomes troubled, it is your own fault. No one else is responsible. You should understand that the fault is yours and it occurred because you did not know how to look at the other person. You must destroy this fault. You should only look at the pure Soul within that person. I have given you the solution: the knowledge that 'I am the pure Soul' and everything else is vyavasthit; scientific circumstantial evidence. (P.229)

After your son marries, it will not help you to start any conflict with his wife. Therefore you must be cautious from the very start. If you all live together, it will cause friction, which will make everyone's life miserable. If you want your children's love, let them live their own life. Your love for each other will grow if you remain apart. When you all live together, your son will obviously side with his wife and not pay attention to what you say. Then your love for each other will dwindle. When your daughter-in-law complains about you to your son, and he sympathizes with her, you will be hurt and all the domestic problems will begin. It is better to be happy and live away from each other. (P. 234)

Questioner : I miss my children who live abroad and keep worrying about them.

Dadashri : The children are having a great time abroad. They do not even think about their mother and here the mother worries about them.

Questioner : The children keep writing to us, asking us to come and live with them abroad.

Dadashri : Yes, but is it in your hands to go? What is wrong with letting things be the way they are? You should live your own life and let them live theirs. Just because you gave birth to them, does it mean they are yours? If they were yours, they would be with you even after death. But, is that possible? (P.235)

There may be fifty people living in the house, but because you cannot understand their individual innate nature (prakruti), you interfere with them. Should you not recognize the differences in their individual nature?

In Satyug, if one person were a rose in a household, then all the other members of that household would also be roses and if in another household, one were a jasmine, they would all be jasmine. These days, a home will have different types of flowers, individuals with distinct characteristics Do you understand my point? The fields of crops of the same type in Satyug have turned into gardens of varied flowers in Kaliyug, the current era of the time cycle. But what can anyone do when people do not know how to look at things? If you do not know how to perceive and accept these differences in nature, you will be hurt. The world does not have this insight. No one is truly bad. All these differences of opinion arise because of one's ego. Your ego stems from not having this insight. If you could perceive things as they are, there is no such thing as pain. I have no conflicts with anyone in this world. I perceive all the different prakrutis; whether one is a rose, a lily, a tulip or any other flower. (P.239)

Because people cannot recognize different prakrutis, I have written the following sentence in a book: "Homes today have become gardens, so one must make the best of it now." If a father is very noble and generous but his son is stingy, he will resent him and try to make the son just like him. This is not possible, because the son has his own distinct personality. Parents attempt to mold their children into replicas of themselves. They should let them blossom on their own. They should know the children's strong points and nurture them instead. Just observe their prakruti. Why must you fight with them?

It is worth getting to know everyone in the garden. When I give this analogy to the parents, they begin to understand and recognize the different prakrutis of their children. Just understand them once and then deal with them accordingly. There will not be any problems if you act according to their prakrutis. Do you not accommodate your friend's prakruti? In the same way you have to look at their prakruti and understand them and deal with them accordingly. Then you will not have any conflicts in the home, but parents nowadays go to extreme to make their children just like themselves. (P.243)

The entire world is in search of knowledge that deals with worldly interactions. This is not a religion, but a way that shows you the art of living in this world. It shows you how to adjust with your wife, your children and everyone else.

These words are such that they bring about a solution to domestic conflicts and bring harmony into people's lives. People search for words that take away their pain, comfort them and help them in their lives. No one has ever shown them such simple and applicable solutions. (P. 247)

SUFFERING DUE TO SUSPICIONS

I had cautioned a man once about his daughter. I told him that the present time is such that living in today's environment has negative effects on people and that his daughter was no exception. He understood what I told him, so when his daughter eloped with someone, he remembered me. He came to see me and told me that whatever I had told him turned out to be true and that had I not explained things to him, he would have killed himself over the matter. This is what the world is like. It is haphazard and people should accept that whatever happens is justice. Is a person to take his or her own life over such matters? No, that would be foolish. People merely hide behind their façades and claim to be noble. (P.249)

A relative of mine had four daughters who were going to college. He was well informed about everything and expressed his concern about his daughters. He told me that since his daughters were now grown up and going to college, he could not trust them. So I told him that he should go to their college and follow them around, but how long could he keep this up. I told him he was foolish in not knowing whom he should trust and whom he should not. Instead he should explain to his daughters that they come from a respectable family and that it was their duty to uphold the reputation of the entire family. Parents should caution their children this way, and after that, whatever happens is correct. They should not be suspicious. So many people harbor suspicions. Those who have more worldly awareness have more suspicions. But where will such suspicion lead them?

Therefore, whatever suspicions arise in your mind, you should eradicate them immediately. You suspect your daughters even when they go out to have simple fun. Do these suspicions allow you to be happy? (P.250)

Do not let suspicions take hold of you even when your daughter comes home late at night. It will be to your advantage to destroy your suspicions. What is the use of such unfounded mental anguish? Nothing can change in just one lifetime. Do not hurt your daughters and sons unnecessarily. Just tell them directly that they should not come home too late because it is not right for young adults of a respectable family to stay out too late. You should talk with them calmly and explain things to them, but you should not have suspicions about who they might be seeing or what they might be doing. If your daughter comes home late again, then again you should caution her in the same way. If you throw her out of the house, there is no telling where she will go. What will you achieve from this? Instead it is to your advantage to resort to a solution that is least destructive. And that is why I have told everyone that even if their daughters come home late, they should let them come in. Some parents are so strict that they will not let their daughters enter the house and dismiss them from outside. These are strange times, full of anguish and suffering. Besides, this is Kaliyug. So you should explain things to them in a calm manner. (P.255)

Questioner : If someone were to be suspicious about us, how should we deal with it?

Dadashri : You should dismiss your thoughts that he has suspicions about you. You should get it out of your mind.

Questioner : Should we ask him why he has these suspicions?

Dadashri : It does not do any good to ask that person. You should not ask. You should immediately realize that there must be some error on your part. Why should anyone have any suspicions about you? (P.256)

The fault is of the sufferer. If you apply this sentence, it will solve all your problems. Who is the one suffering? Is it the person who doubts or is it the person who is being doubted? Just ask yourself this. (P.257)

HOW MUCH INHERITANCE FOR YOUR CHILDREN?

Questioner : What happens when because of our merit karma, we get more money than we need?

Dadashri : You should spend it well and not keep too much aside for your children. Once you fulfill your duty to educate them and give them a good upbringing and when they are well established, you need not give them financial support. Just remember that only your merit karma comes with you in the next life. Only money that is spent for anyone other than your blood relatives will bind merit karma. (P.259)

Questioner : Is a person able to take any money with him to his next life?

Dadashri : What can he take now? He has used up whatever he had in this life. Now only the knowledge of his real Self can help him. If he comes to me and attains this, then he will accomplish everything. It is not too late in his life to do this. It is better late than never.

What are you able to carry forward into your next life? Only that which you have done for the benefit of others will help you; that is your real savings for your next life. Everything that you have done for yourself, your own pleasures and comforts have all gone to waste in the gutter. (P.260)

A man asked me whether this meant that we should not give anything to his children. I told him that he should give everything that he inherited from his own parents. Any surplus should be spent on helping others.

Questioner : According to Indian law whatever I inherited has to go to my children. Whereas, I am free to do whatever I wish with my own earnings.

Dadashri : Yes, you can decide to use it the way you want to. Therefore, leave aside whatever you earn yourself and use it to help others. Only that will carry forward with you into the next life. After attaining this Gnan, you still have one or two more births remaining and you will need something for yourself. Even when you go out of town, you take some food along with you, so will you not need something for the next life?

All you need to give to your son is the house you live in, if you own it. You should let your son know that he will become the owner of the house only upon your death. When you die, everything will be his, but if he does not live properly and misbehaves, then you will have to ask him and his wife to leave. But as long as you are alive the property is yours. You should also make a will. Give to your son, whatever you inherited from your own father. Do not divulge all your assets to him. If he thinks that you have half the amount of what you actually have, let him think that. He may have expectations of inheriting that amount from you. Let him be with his greed until the end. And in his greed, he will instruct his wife to take good care of you. Live your life with pride. Pass on your inheritance to your son. (P.262)

No one is allowed to take anything along with him. They burn us on the funeral pyre when we go. If you leave an excessive amount of wealth behind, the children will think that there is no need for them to work for a living. They will lose themselves to a life of alcohol and other vices; they will fall into the company of alcoholics. So you should give to your children, but within limits. If you leave them an excessive amount of money, they will end up abusing it. Make it so that they will have to work for their living. If they are idle, they will fall prey to all kinds of vices. (P.263).

If your son likes a particular business, help him establish it. Help him borrow about fifty percent from the bank and you may provide the rest. Let him make regular payments on the loan from the bank. This will make him financially responsible. (P. 266)

Help him just enough to get started and use the rest of your wealth to give happiness to others. How can you give happiness to others? By appeasing their hearts. It is this wealth that will follow you into your next life. It does not come in the form of cash, but in the form of an 'overdraft' from this life. By helping the needy people and soothing their sorrows, you will acquire a 'draft' for use in your next life. So use your money wisely. Do not worry about anything. Eat well and do not be miserly when it comes to food. Enhance other people's lives and collect all the overdrafts. (P. 271)

I told a young man that his father had worked very hard and had deprived himself of good clothing and luxuries to accumulate a lot of wealth for him. He told me that I did not know his father. He told me that his father was such a shrewd man that if he could, he would take all his wealth and in addition borrow millions more to take with him to his next life. When he shared this with me I understood what I needed to learn. (P.272)

A man and his wife, who wanted to pursue a spiritual life, relinquished all their wealth to their only son. One should never do this. You should never tell your son that all your wealth is his, too early in his life. What can happen in situations like this? Initially the son may take care of his parents but a day will come when he will tell them to go their own way. Rather than live a life of regret, it is better not to let go of your wealth completely. (P.274)

If a father tells his son that he will inherit all his wealth, and the son tells him that he has no expectations of receiving his wealth and that he is free to use his own money as he pleases, then the son has the certificate and has good spiritual insight. (P.288)

SUFERRING LIFE AFTER LIFE BECAUSE OF ATTACHMENT

Questioner : Who is to know whether our children will still be ours when they grow up?

Dadashri : Of course, no one knows. Does anything remain yours forever? Even your body does not remain yours. It is taken away from you. How long can anything that does not belong to you, remain with you? (P.292)

Because parents have tremendous attachment for their

Generation Gap

children, when they hear their child utter the words 'mommy' and 'daddy', they become further entrenched in their attachment. Even when the child pulls the father's moustache, the father does not say anything. Children are very useful. They act as go-betweens when their parents quarrel. There will always be quarrels between husbands and wives, so how does a child act as the peacemaker? If the father is sulking, the mother will tell the child to relay messages to him. The father 'melts' and forgets everything when he hears the word 'daddy', as though it were some magic mantra! (P.292)

No man is truly a son to anyone in this world. Is there anywhere in this world, a son, who after being severely scolded continuously by his father for hours, tells his father he still feels oneness with him? Generally, half an hour's worth of rebuke will make the son break relations with his father (P.293)

If you are swayed and delighted with your child when he endearingly calls you 'daddy', you should understand that the joy you are experiencing is borrowed happiness, which will have to be repaid in the form of sorrow some later time. When your son grows up and insults you, you will feel sorrow and pain, and that sorrow will be the repayment of the borrowed happiness. So be cautious from the very beginning. I have stopped borrowing such happiness a long time ago. When infinite bliss exists, where is the need to seek any temporary happiness? (P.295)

A young man asked his seventy-year-old neighbour who had been very depressed, why now she was saying that she wished she were dead. The man inquired what had happened. She told him that it was because her son had started quarreling with her and wanted her out of the house. In the past this same son of hers was very dear to her and was a source of lot of comfort. This is how the accounts of attachment and abhorrence unfold in life.(P.297)

Penance is necessary on the path of liberation. In these times, one does not have to go outside of his home seeking penance, as did the aspirants of the past. Penance readily occurs in the form of conflict with other family members. You should consider yourselves fortunate that such instruments of penance are found in your own homes and view them as instruments of benefit for your spiritual development.

Even Lord Mahavir, in search of penance, had to leave his kingdom, to go to areas inhabited by uncivilized tribes. You, on the other hand, find such penance within your own homes. When a son speaks rudely to his father, the father thinks to himself that had he known that his life would be reduced to this, he would never have married and had children. But unfortunately one does not come to this realization until it is too late.

Questioner : Does this mean that when we encounter unfavorable circumstances, our focused awareness (upayog) should be towards the Self?

Dadashri : All unfavorable circumstances in life are beneficial for your spiritual progress. They are vitamin for the Soul. In times of crisis, does one not withdraw into his real Self? If someone were to insult you right now, your focus would not remain in the external world and you would become one with your Soul. This is applicable only for those who have acquired the knowledge of the Self. (P.298)

Questioner : Who will take care of us in our old age?

Dadashri : Why do you have such expectations? It would be enough if your children do not abuse you. Do not expect to be cared for in your old age. Only about five percent of children take care of their parents; the rest mistreat them. (P.299)

A son tells his father that he is tired of listening to his constant nagging and that he wants his share of the inheritance. The father in turn tells him that he will not give a single penny of his hard-earned money to him because he had been a constant source of grief for him. The son tells his father that the wealth belonged to his grandfather and that he will take him to court for his share. This proves that the children are not really yours. (P.302)

If a father insults his son and fights with him for an hour, what will the son do? The son will challenge his father's authority. He may even take his father to court over issues regarding his inheritance. Will the father still worry about his son then? His worries will cease once his attachment for his son leaves. Anxieties and troubles occur to those who have attachment. (P.305)

If a man's brother-in-law were ill in the hospital, he would visit him at least a dozen times, whereas if his own father were ill, he would probably only see him a couple of times. Who influences this kind of behavior in him? His wife pressures him into seeing her brother. She turns the 'key' and he becomes oblivious to everything else. The wives influence this whole world. (P.307)

A son is generally quite good as long as he does not meet his 'guru' (the wife). But it is inevitable; he is bound to meet her, whether she is Indian or otherwise, and once this happens, the control will no longer be in the hands of the parents. So the parents should manage the reins properly, and let go where necessary.
(P.307)

Questioner : If we hated someone in our past life, will we have to meet the same individual in this life to repay the debt?

Dadashri : Not necessarily. Debts are not paid off in that way. When you bind vengeance, you create raag-dwesh from within. If you had animosity towards your son in this life, you may wonder when the two of you will reunite to pay off that debt. It may even be that the son comes into your home as a cat that scratches you even when you offer it some milk. This is how accounts are paid off. This is a world of cause and effect. Sooner or later the causes will have to be paid off. Many children come with such intentions of revenge that they make their parents' lives miserable. Does this not happen? (P.314)

Questioner : I have three daughters and I worry about their future. What shall I do?

Dadashri : Instead of worrying about their future, it would be better for you to secure a 'safe side' by daily application of what I have been teaching you. Your worries about their future are detrimental. Your greatest solution is to secure this 'safe-side' for yourself daily. (P.324)

Become and live as a trustee for your children. You should not have worries or anxieties about their marriage. (P.326)

Your daughters have come with their own karma. You need not worry about them. Just take good care of them. They already come with a suitor for themselves. Do you need to go around telling people to give birth to a son for your daughters? They already come prepared. When your daughter becomes of age, you become anxious, but you do not know that somewhere in this world there is a suitable boy already waiting for her. So stop worrying and sleep soundly. (P.326)

Worries create obstructing karmas (antaraya karma) and they only serve to prolong the work at hand. If a friend tells you about an eligible boy for your daughter who is of age, you should make arrangements for them to meet. But if you worry, your anxiety will just be another obstacle for you to overcome. Just ask yourself whether anything in this world is in your hands. Do you have any control over any situation? Do you even have control over your own bowels that you can go to the bathroom at will? Is there not some other force at work behind everything? (P.329)

Even on his deathbed, a man worries about the future of his unmarried daughter and so he passes away in a state of adverse internal meditation. This will result in him taking birth in the animal kingdom, where his life will be filled with pain. What else can he expect for not living his life, the way it should be lived? (P.331)

CONSIDER YOURSELF BLESSED FOR NOT HAVING CHILDREN

Dadashri : Do you ever worry?

Questioner : Generally I do not worry. I have everything, but at times I wished I had a child.

Dadashri : It is like having a lot of food but no one (son or daughter) to eat it. Yes that too can be a problem! (P.336)

In certain lifetimes, those who are born with great merit karma will have no children. It is because karmas determine whether or not a couple will have children. Consider yourself very fortunate that you do not have any children in this life. Who says that a childless couple is unfortunate? A man told me that his wife constantly griped about not having children. I then met with his wife and explained the reality of things to her. She finally understood the blessings of being childless. (P.337)

If a child is born to a couple after many years of waiting, the father becomes overjoyed. But if that child goes away, then the father will suffer just as much. So you should understand that the one that comes will also have to leave, and when that happens, what will become of you? Instead it would be better to be aware about the nature of things, so that later on you do not suffer disappointment. (P.339)

Children are really our accounts of raag and dwesh, not money. Raag and dwesh is a consequence of relationships from our past lives. As a consequence of these accounts of raag and dwesh, the children will harass the father to no end. Even the great King Shrenik in the time of Lord Mahavir was tortured in prison by his own son.

People complain about having no children. What is all the fuss about having children when they make their parents' lives miserable? What use are they? Was there ever a life in which you did not have children? You have finally, with so much difficulty, managed to attain this human life and that too being without a child, so use it to your advantage. Search for that which will lead you to your liberation. (P. 341)

Questioner : Last year I lost my only son and I suffered a lot. I want to know what I did in my previous life to deserve this.

Dadashri : This is simply a matter of accounts. His time with you is dependant on this account. Once the account is over, he leaves. This is the law.

Questioner : When a child dies immediately after birth, does it mean that the child had just that much of an account with us?

Dadashri : The account of raag and dwesh of the child with his parents is very precise. When he leaves he makes them suffer terribly. Some accounts are such that the child will die only after leaving his parents with enormous medical bills. (P.348)

When parents grieve for their dead child, it brings suffering to the child. People do all sorts of things in ignorance. You should accept things and stay calm. Why all the unnecessary fuss?

Generation Gap

Everyone will lose his child at some point in time.

I too, had a boy and a girl who died in infancy. They were our guests who came and left. They were not our property and they did not belong to us. Will we not also have to leave, one day? It is our duty to give happiness to those who are living and dependent on us. Those who are gone are gone forever, so stop crying for them. What people do instead is keep remembering those who have gone and neglect the ones who are living and present in front of them. This is how people fail to carry out their duties. If you lose a lot of money, what will you do? Will you torture yourself over it?

Questioner : No I would forget about it.

Dadashri : Yes, all suffering stems from ignorance. In reality nobody is a father or a son. There is no point in worrying about the loss of your children. It is only for your parents that you must have such worries, because they were the ones who took care of you and nurtured you. The mother took care of you for nine months and the father supported you throughout your life. (P.351)

Whenever you remember your child, just say a prayer to Dada and tell Him that you are placing your child in His hands. Ask for his salvation and your child will be cared for. Do not allow yourself to shed any tears. Being a Jain, you should know the prayers for the departed soul. It will do you no good to break down emotionally; it will only bring suffering to your loved one that has departed. You are wise and you are intelligent, so whenever you think of your son, pray for his salvation. It does not matter whether you pray to Krupaludev (a Gnani Purush) or Dada Bhagwan, because although their physical bodies are different, there is no difference between their souls. They may appear different to the eye, but in the elemental form they are the same.

And the same would apply when you say your prayers to Lord Mahavir or Lord Krishna. You should repeatedly pray for the salvation of the ones with whom you shared joys and sorrows during their lifetime. You have such good intentions for others, so why would you not do the same for your own family? (P. 353)

Questioner : Dada, how many children did you have?

Dadashri : We had a boy and a girl. In 1928, when the son was born I celebrated his birth by distributing pendas (sweets) to all my friends and when he died three years later, I did the same thing. At first everyone thought that another son was born to us. I waited until they finished the pendas and then I told them: "The little boy who was a guest in my house, has now left." We greet them with love and respect when they come, so we should do the same when they leave. Everyone became very upset and started scolding me. Such scolding is inappropriate. We should show respect when they leave. After that, a little girl was born to us and she too died in infancy. She also received the same welcome and farewell. Now there is no one left except Hiraba (Dada's wife) and myself. (P.360)

After this, Hiraba would worry about who would look after us in our old age, since we had no children. I told her that the children of today only cause more trouble than what it is worth. I asked her what she would do if she had an alcoholic son. She realized later on that what I was saying was true when she witnessed the problems other parents had with their children.

Can anything that does not belong to you ever become yours? Your worries are unfounded. When your very own body does not belong to you, how can your children belong to you?
(P.362)

Questioner : My only son has alienated himself from me.

Dadashri : Even if you had three sons, they may have done the same thing. And if not, you yourself would have to leave them one day. Even if you all lived together, you would still have to leave them one day. So why bother about it? What about the children you left behind in your past life? Do you know where they are?

Questioner : God only knows.

Dadashri : You have no idea about what is happening with the children of your past life. And this is what happens to you with your children of this life. When will you wake up? Instead start thinking about your liberation or else you will end up being born into a lower life form. If in this human life you allow yourself to suffer because of external circumstances or if you take your life, you will reincarnate into the animal kingdom, or even hell. Does the prospect of a lower life form appeal to you? (P. 363)

In all your previous lives you have suffered terribly. You forget the suffering from your previous lives and begin to suffer again in this one. You abandoned your children in your previous life and in this life you bring forth new ones. (P.364)

RELATIONSHIPS: ARE THEY RELATIVE OR REAL?

All these relationships are temporary. You must conduct your interactions carefully. These are all relative relationships and they will remain as relative as you keep them. The definition of a worldly life is that it will give back exactly whatever you put into it.

You may believe that because he is your son, he will be loyal to you, but just because he is your son does not mean that he will not go against you. The Soul never becomes a father or a son. These relationships are merely accounts of give and take. But do not go home and tell your father that he is not your father. In the worldly sense he is still your father. (P.370)

All these relatives are temporary adjustments. As long as you adjust to them, everything will be fine. Your intentions should be to preserve the relationship, even though others try to destroy it. Try to keep things as stable as you can, but when you feel that your efforts are in vain, then you can let go. As long as possible, try to keep things together. (P.371)

In your worldly interactions, you should conduct yourself as though you are an actor in a play. Internally you should remain detached from the situation. Do everything that you have to do, but without emotional involvement. A mother who hugs her child dearly may do so to the point of smothering it and then naturally the child becomes irritated. It is the ignorant that display such possessive behavior. Whereas the Gnani Purush remains detached from all worldly interactions and so everyone remains happy with him.

From the Gnani's perspective, it is a worldly matter when a girl gets married and it is also a worldly matter when she becomes a widow. It is not real. Both the situations are relative and no one has the ability to change them. People agonize over the death of their young son-in-law. They become so distraught that they have to seek medical help. All such emotions and reactions are due to attachment and abhorrence. It is all because people have not understood worldly life as worldly life and nothing else; they have not understood that the worldly life is temporary.

You may have to scold your child and at times you may even have to say something to your wife. But you should do so in a make-believe way, as if you are an actor in a play, without any emotional involvement from within. (P.378)

ALL RELATIONSHIPS ARE MERELY GIVE AND TAKE

If your wife and child were truly yours, then they would

share all your pain and suffering. If you were to become paralyzed, would your son share your paralysis? No one can take away your pain; these are all merely your accounts from your previous life. As a son, you will only receive from your father, precisely what is owed to you from your previous life. (P.384)

A mother beats one of her children although he does nothing wrong, while she pampers another who is mischievous and unmanageable. All of them are her children and yet she treats them all differently, why?

Questioner : Each has brought different karmas with him.

Dadashri : All the accounts are being repaid. The mother wants to treat all her children equally, but she is not able to do so. How is it possible for her to do so, when they each have different accounts with her? The children on the other hand complain about their mother taking sides. This is the cause of disputes in the world today.

Questioner : Why does the mother feel the way she does towards the child she beats repeatedly for no reason?

Dadashri : It is because she has some revenge for him from her past life. And for the one she pampers, she has an account of attachment from her previous life. The world, however expects her to treat all her children the same. (P.389)

Many children look after their parents so well that they put their parents before themselves. It is not because of the children that this happens. It is because of the merit karma of the parents that they are treated so well. Everything is according to our own accounts. We suffer because of our own faults. Why did we have to be born in this Kaliyug? Was there not a Satyug when everyone lived harmoniously? In Kaliyug everyone we encounter will be awkward and difficult. If your son is good, then his wife or his in-laws will be bad. In this way the fire of discontentment keeps burning in all the homes. (P.397)

Questioner : If a mango tree bears fruit, all the mangos will taste the same, whereas children of the same parents all have different qualities of thought, speech and conduct. Why is that so?

Dadashri : Even the mangos from the same tree will differ from one another. You do not have the power to discriminate between the subtle differences. Each mango differs in taste and appearance. Even the leaves are different. The aroma maybe the same, but they all differ. This is because the law of nature dictates that whenever there is a change in space, there will be differences. Changes occur because of change in space. Do you understand? (P.400)

Questioner : There is a common saying that all these families are simply a succession of a series of sons, grandsons, great-grandsons, etc.

Dadashri : Yes. They are all acquainted with each other. Your entire circle of acquaintances will stay with you. They all have similar qualities and because of raag and dwesh they are born close to each other. They come together to settle accounts of raag and dwesh. All that you see with your eyes is an illusion. From the perspective of real knowledge, things are not as they appear to be. (P. 403)

Questioner : Do people take birth because of their karmas?

Dadashri : Yes, the fact that he is fair, tall, short, white or black is all because of his karma. Whereas people conclude that since the child has a nose just like his father's, that he will inherit all his father's qualities. So this would mean that since the father becomes Lord Krishna, does that mean that his son too will be Lord Krishna? So many such 'Lord Krishnas' have been born. All Self-Realized beings can be regarded as Lord Krishna, but have any of their sons also become Lord Krishnas? So therefore such talks lack understanding. (P.404)

If the traits of the father were to be transmitted to the children, all of them would receive the same qualities and in the same amount. It is because of the acquaintances of the father's previous life, that he has such traits. His traits match the traits of those he knew in his previous life. If his acquaintances from his past life had similar intellect and thinking as his; then these acquaintances will be born as his children in this life. And that is why their characteristics and personalities appear to be similar. But in reality these attributes are their very own. The scientists believe that it is because of genetics, but in reality he comes with his own characteristics. A person may turn out to be a drunk or a lecher. The circumstances that he surrounded himself with in his previous life are what he will find in this life. This is exactly how it is. Nothing is inherited from the parents. It merely appears that way. In reality these are all his acquaintances from the past life.

(P.404)

Questioner : That means that we are all here for repayment of previous accounts. Once these accounts of raag and dwesh we have with everyone from our past life are paid off, they go their own way.

Dadashri : Yes, it all gets paid off. I am disclosing this exact science for the first time with such clarity. To clarify this further, if your father is hot-tempered and you take after him, then why is your brother so calm? If you inherited the qualities of your father, then why did your brother not inherit the same qualities? People do not understand this, which is why they draw all sorts of wrong conclusions and believe what appears on the surface to be the truth. This is indeed worth the understanding; it is a very profound matter. It goes much deeper and beyond what I have said so far. Even God himself cannot give or pass on anything. Everything is simply based on the give and take of accounts. (P.409)

The Soul can never become a father, a mother, a son, a wife, a daughter or a husband to anyone. All relationships are merely connections from past lives. Everything comes together because of the effect of past karmas. Everyone is under an illusion. Furthermore the reality is not visible. If it were, then there would be no discord in this world at all. But here people fight and argue in a matter of minutes.

Everything in this world is an illusion; things are not exactly as they appear. Only the Soul, the real Self is permanent, everything else is temporary.

In this current time cycle of Kaliyug, do not have any expectations of any kind. There are terrible times ahead and there is no telling when you will attain a human life again, so concentrate on attaining your salvation. (P.410)

PART II
CHILDREN'S CONDUCT TOWARDS PARENTS

DADASHRI'S SATSANG WITH TEENAGERS

Questioner : What qualities should an ideal student have?

Dadashri : The student should keep everyone happy, both at home and at school. He should also concentrate on his studies.
(P.419)

Have you ever killed any insects?

Questioner : Yes.

Dadashri : Where?

Questioner : In our garden.

Dadashri : What sort of insects?

Questioner : All kinds.

Dadashri : Would you ever kill a human infant?

Questioner : No.

Dadashri : No, you cannot kill anyone's child.

Questioner : No.

Dadashri : Why is that? Since you killed those insects, will you now make an insect for me? I will give a reward of a hundred thousand dollars if you or anyone else can make an insect for me. Will you make one? It is not possible right?

Questioner : No.

Dadashri : So then how can you kill them? Can even a scientist create an insect?

Questioner : No.

Dadashri : So then you cannot kill anything that you cannot create yourself. You can make this chair; you can make all such things, and those things you can destroy. Do you understand?

Questioner : Yes.

Dadashri : So what will you do from now on?

Questioner : I will not kill any more insects.

Dadashri : Do you think that insects have a fear of dying? Do they run away when you try to kill them?

Questioner : Yes.

Dadashri : Then how can you kill them? All these wheat and barley crops do not become frightened when you harvest them. They do not run away. Does the eggplant run away when you cut it with a knife?

Questioner : No.

Dadashri : Then you can cook it and eat it. Are you afraid of dying?

Questioner : Yes.

Dadashri : So in the same way, the insects too have the same fear. (P.423)

Dadashri : Are you married?

Questioner : No.

Dadashri : Do you have sexual thoughts about anyone?

Questioner : Sometimes...

Dadashri : Beware. The consequences of sexual thoughts and actions about anyone other than your spouse are very grave. You will be digging a very deep hole for yourself, from which you will not be able to climb out. So walk very carefully and be very cautious. You are still young and that is why I am cautioning you. If you were an old man, I would not say anything.

Questioner : Yes Dada, I understand. I will try my best not to harbour sexual thoughts.

Dadashri : Do not even entertain such thoughts. If you feel sexual attraction towards any woman, you must instantly do pratikraman; ask for forgiveness from Dada Bhagwan. (P.425)

Questioner : What should I do when my mom and dad get angry with me?

Dadashri : Just say 'Jai Sat Chit Anand'. And keep saying, 'Jai Sat Chit Anand, Jai Sat Chit Anand' and they will eventually calm down. (P.433)

If dad is quarrelling with mom, and the children start saying, 'Jai Sat Chit Anand', the parents will become embarrassed. Just press the panic button that will start the alarm, 'Jai Sat Chit Anand', and the quarrel will come to an abrupt end. (P.433)

Conduct yourself in such a way that everyone at home is happy with you. If they hurt you, settle the dispute with equanimity; without attachment or abhorrence and try to make them all happy.

Then watch the love that develops between you. If you keep behaving negatively, you are destroying the foundation of their love and eventually it will not be there. (P. 437)

Questioner : Why do our elders get angry so quickly?

Dadashri : When a car gets old and junky, it will overheat quickly. This does not happen to new cars. It is the same thing with the elderly. When a car overheats, do we not have to let it cool down? In the same way, they may have had some conflict outside the home, so that when they come home you will see a disgruntled expression on their face. At that time you cannot say to them that they always look disgruntled whenever you look at them. You merely have to understand that they may have encountered some difficulty and so you should just leave them alone until they calm down. (P.444)

To look after our elders is the highest religion. What is the duty of today's youth? It should be to take care of their elders. Helping 'tow' these old cars will ensure that in your old age you will find someone to tow you when you break down. You will receive what you give. If you are abusive all the time towards your elderly parents, you will encounter similar abuse when you become old. You are free to do what you want. (P.445)

SELECTION OF A WIFE

You cannot change what destiny has in store for you. If you are destined to marry, you cannot avoid it. Even if you decide that you do not want to marry, you will not be able to avoid marriage.

Questioner : Will the inner intent and design (bhaav) we make in this life come to fruition in our next life?

Dadashri : Yes, whatever bhaav you have made in this life will come into effect in the next life. But you cannot change anything in this life, nobody can. Even the Lord himself cannot change anything for Himself! You made the bhaav to marry in your past life, so marriage is inevitable for you in this life. Whatever plan you made in your past life, is what will come into effect in this life. (P. 449)

Just as people cannot live without defecating, they cannot live without getting married. If mentally you are a bachelor there is no problem, but if your mind is filled with marriage, you cannot avoid marriage. People cannot live in solitude. They need others around them. Who can exist in solitude? Only the Gnani Purush can exist in sólitude, because he is absolutely independent. He has no need for any kind of support.

Human beings cannot survive without human warmth and security. If we tell someone to sleep alone in a very large and expensive bungalow, would he like it? Man needs human warmth and security, which is why he gets married. It is not wrong to get married. It is the law of nature.

Just be spontaneous and natural about marriage. Keep in your mind that you want to get married to someone from a good family, and when the circumstances arrive, you should get married. But what is the point of becoming anxious and restless before the time is right? Do you want to run around unnecessarily before your time is right?

Questioner : No, only when the time is right.

Dadashri : Yes. You are in need of a wife and the wife is in need of you. (P.450)

Questioner : If some of your young followers say they do not wish to get married, what advice do you give to them in private?

Dadashri : In private, I tell them to get married. I tell them that they should get married, so that it will help reduce the number of unmarried girls and I also tell them that I do not have any problems with those who marry. This path of liberation is open and available for married people also; there are no restrictions here that exclude married people.

But these young adults have discovered for themselves that there are lots of problems in a marriage. They tell me that they have seen how happy their own parents are and that they do not want that kind of happiness. (P.451)

Do not pressure your son into marriage or else he will blame you for ruining his life. The truth of the matter is that the son will not know how to get along with his wife, so he will end up blaming you. (P.453)

If you have a girl in mind for your son, tell him that you approve of her and that if he also approves her, you can pursue the matter further. If he does not like the girl, then you should just drop the matter. You must first get his consent; otherwise he will keep blaming you. (P.453)

Questioner : Is it a sin to marry a person you are in love with?

Dadashri : No. A temporary love marriage is considered a sin. Such a marriage would only last for one or two years. A life-long love marriage however, is acceptable. If one wishes to marry, he should only marry once. People should not have too many relationships; such a situation would take them to hell.(P.455)

A father questions the integrity of his son's relationship with his girlfriend. But when the son becomes very defensive and abusive towards him, the father recognizes that the son is not ready to accept his advice and that it would be better to let him learn from

Generation Gap 73

his own experience. Later his son sees his girlfriend with another boy at the movies and he immediately realizes that his father was right all along. (P.457)

Questioner : What is the difference between attachment (moha) and love (prem)?

Dadashri : Have you seen moths hovering around an open flame and eventually destroy themselves in it? They destroy their own lives. That is called moha (infatuation). Love however, is everlasting. Nevertheless there is still some attachment in it. But the marriage which lasts, is more than just attachment or infatuation. (P.458)

For example, in a relationship where there is infatuation, if one of the partners develops a hideous boil on the face, the other partner would find it repulsive to look at him or her and the infatuation would diminish. With love, even if one partner develops innumerable boils on his or her body, it would not affect the other at all. Find yourself such a love or do not get married at all. Otherwise you will have to deal with the consequences of infatuation and attachment.

If your spouse sulks, you will come to despise his looks. If he says something pleasant to you, you will like him, but when he says something bitter and spiteful, you begin to dislike him. (P.459)

Questioner : How can I stop dating?

Dadashri : You should stop it. Decide to do this right now. It is your duty to stop doing something wrong as soon as you realize it. You must stop dating because from our Gnan you now know that you will create causes for future suffering.

If you are pure you will find a spouse who is pure. That is vyavasthit, and it is precise. (P.459)

Questioner : I do not discriminate between colors. If she is a good person, what difference does it make whether she is an American or an Indian?

Dadashri : No. Do not even think about getting involved with an American girl. You have seen the relationship between your father and mother. Do they ever have disputes?

Questioner : Yes, they have disputes.

Dadashri : But when that happens, does your mother ever walk out on your father?

Questioner : No, she does not.

Dadashri : On the other hand a non-Indian wife will put all the blame on you, threaten you and leave you. An Indian wife will always stay with you, through thick and thin. I am trying to make you understand by warning you about the consequences. Do not get involved with a non-Indian girl or else you will regret it.

If you have an Indian wife, no matter how much you fight with one another, things will always go back to the way they were.

Questioner : Yes that is right.

Dadashri : So therefore, decide that you will only marry an Indian girl. Then it does not matter whether she is a Brahmin, a Jain or a Vaishnav. (P.461)

Questioner : What are the benefits of marrying within one's own caste?

Dadashri : If you marry someone of your own caste, you will have similar traits and a mutual understanding. There are some inherent idiosyncrasies in each caste. These differences may be small, but they will also be the cause of minor frictions between the two of you and sometimes these differences may even be drastic. For example, if you like ghee (clarified butter) on your khichadi (rice dish) and if you marry someone from another caste who generally does not use ghee, she will be reluctant to use ghee in her cooking. So problems will occur frequently because of such small differences. However, if she is of your own caste, the chances of such minor frictions are less. Do you understand? Even the language she might speak will differ to your own and she will complain that you do not speak well.

Questioner : You say that when one marries within his own caste there will not be any conflicts, but we see conflicts in same caste marriages also. What is the reason for this?

Dadashri : Yes, there are conflicts, but they are also resolved. They enjoy each other's company, whereas with a spouse from another caste, mutual dislikes will set in and they will grow over time. This leads to an increasing sense of frustration and tension, for which he has no solution and he is not able to express to anyone either. I have seen many couples suffering in these situations. (P.463)

Nowadays it does not present a problem to marry outside of one's caste. In the past it was a problem. (P.467)

Questioner : But it is not in our hands if they marry an American!

Dadashri : Although it is not in your hands does that mean you have to let it go completely? You must tell your children that they cannot go around with American girls and that it is not good for them. Such repeated coaxing done without raag-dwesh will have positive results. Otherwise if you let it go, he will think that you approve and he will continue dating. What is wrong with telling him? If you are walking through a bad neighborhood, do you not take extra care with your wallet? Likewise, when there is potential danger, you must warn your children. (P.468)

Questioner : What kind of qualities should we look for in a spouse before entering into a marriage?

Dadashri : You do not need to look at them too critically. When you meet your potential suitor and you feel no attraction towards him or her, then you should not proceed further. It is not necessary to look for any other qualities. It is the initial attraction that is important.

Questioner : What sort of attraction?

Dadashri : From the first glance, when you see the person, there is an inner attraction. You are drawn to that person, just as you would when you see an object in a shop. You will not be able to purchase that object unless you are attracted to it. Attraction is based on previous accounts. In the absence of such an account, no one can marry. There has to be an attraction. (P.479)

Women are ridiculed when they are asked to parade themselves in front of their potential suitors for approval. What a terrible insult and indignity towards women!! Nowadays, the boys are very critical when selecting their potential spouse. They will comment on the woman's height, her looks, her build etc. I once heard a boy talking like this and I rebuked him for doing so. The fool! What audacity! I told him that at one time, his mother too was a bride to be. What kind of a man was he to insult women in this way?

I ask these young men, whether they think that these young women are cattle that they are inspecting them in this manner. People scrutinize cattle in this way. (P.480)

Do you know when these women will take their revenge

for insulting them? Do you know what consequences you men will have to endure for your actions?

Currently there is an increase in the number of females and consequently their value has declined. This is all nature's doing. Now when will the results of men's actions come into fruition? It will be when there is a decrease in the female population and a surplus of men. It is when the women will be making a decision as to what kind of a husband they want. The women will ask for swayamwvar (a custom prevalent in India hundreds of years ago, when invitations would be sent to all eligible young men by the father whose daughter was of a marriageable age, inviting them to present themselves at the reception of swayamvar. The girl would then place a garland of flowers around the neck of the suitor of her choice). At the swayamvar there would be a hundred or so suitors for just one girl. They would come to the swayamvar all decked out in the finest of clothes. As they line up for her inspection, they twirl their moustaches in a gesture of confidence, each thinking to himself that he will be the chosen one. They incline their heads forward, as she walks along the ranks, but she passes them by without a second glance. She does this until her heart leaps at the sight of the man she feels attraction for and she garlands him. The others walk away with their heads downcast, looking hopeless and foolish. This is their repayment for their own past foolishness. (P.482)

Nowadays marriages are reduced to contracts of dowry. Love has been set aside and marriages have become a commodity of monetary dealings. The groom's parents will demand a dowry in exchange for their son's hand in marriage. The marriage is not allowed to proceed, until the demands are met. (P.486)

SELECTION OF A HUSBAND

There is nothing but dependency in this world. No one is

independent. No one is truly free. A father is not willing to let his daughter live at home forever, and he insists that she must get married. When she marries she has to live with her in-laws, who constantly nag and criticize her. She asks herself how she is going to deal with such a nagging mother-in-law. When she married, she only expected to gain a husband and not such a large extended family of in laws. (P.490)

There is nothing wrong with marriage. You can get married, but do so with the understanding that there will be problems in the marriage. One has no choice but to get married. Only in certain cases there are exceptions when a girl had the deep inner intent in her past life to remain celibate. Her situation will be different. If you accept from the very beginning, that in a marriage, one will be faced with many difficult situations, then you will not be faced with any unpleasant surprises. If, however you have a very idealistic view of marriage, you will be disappointed and miserable. It is not an easy task to enter your mother-in-law's house. In rare cases one might come across a husband whose parents are not living.
(P.490)

People that are civilized do not fight. They always manage to sleep peacefully without bickering. It is the uncivilized ones who argue and fight relentlessly with each other. (P.492)

Questioner : We don't go to any parties where they serve alcohol and meat, but we do go to parties given by our friends, whose parents all know one another and who do not serve alcohol or meat.

Dadashri : But what do you get out of it?

Questioner : Enjoyment. It's a lot of fun!

Dadashri : Enjoyment? There is even enjoyment in eating.

Generation Gap

But while eating, you should tell yourself that you need to exercise some control. Then gradually you will really enjoy the food. It is because you do not restrict yourself that you do not enjoy your food. You keep searching for enjoyment in other things.

Questioner : Should we allow our children to go to these parties? And how many times a year should we let them go?

Dadashri : People have learnt from experience and have come to the conclusion that it is always better for girls to listen to their parents and act according to their parents' wishes. And after marriage they should comply with the wishes of their husband.

Questioner : Should boys do the same? Should they also have to listen to their parents?

Dadashri : Even boys must go along with their parents' wishes. With boys, you can be a little more liberal and more lenient. Your son can stay out late at night even if he goes alone, but can a girl walk around alone late in the night?

Questioner : No, a girl would be afraid.

Dadashri : It is fine to be liberal with boys. Girls shouldn't have so much freedom because in general they are afraid to stay out late. If you run into problems now, you will ruin your future happiness. Your parents refuse to allow you to go out late, to protect you from any unhappy consequences in the future. Your parents caution you because they do not want you to ruin your future. (P.498)

Questioner : It is usually the boy in an Indian family that is favored by his parents who generally feel that the daughters will eventually get married and become part of another family, while the boys will bring home money and support them. This makes the girls feel unwanted and unloved.

Dadashri : A girl is wrong to think that her parents do not love her. All parents love their children. This misunderstanding on her part will hurt her parents, who believe they have undergone great hardship to raise their children.

Questioner : So why do I feel that my parents do not love me?

Dadashri : So many girls ask this question. Such thoughts are easily suppressed when they are young, but as they grow up, how do they deal with such feelings of unworthiness?

They acquire an intellect that is molded and influenced by external factors. This wrong intellect creates a wrong understanding. And it is this wrong understanding that makes her, as well as those around her, suffer. (P.502)

Questioner : Nowadays girls are not ready to marry at an early age.

Dadashri : Yes, they are not ready, but even then it is better for them to get married at an early age. As soon as they finish their studies they should get married. Even if they get married first and later, perhaps in another year or so, complete their education, there would be no problem. Once she becomes bound by marriage, her life will run smoothly. Otherwise, in her later life she will suffer hardship. (P.504)

Dadashri : When you talk about being attracted to friends, are you referring to male friends or female friends?

Questioner : Both.

Dadashri : Boyfriends too?

Questioner : Yes, both.

Dadashri: It is fine. You have to stay in equanimity; without raag or dwesh with them and you should always be on your guard and not lose control of yourself. Those who want to be celibate and attain liberation must have as little contact with the opposite sex as possible. Do you agree?

Questioner: Yes.

Dadashri: Do you desire liberation now?

Questioner: Yes, I do.

Dadashri: So why are you mingling with boys? It is acceptable for you to keep the company of girls. You can go out with them and have a good time. (P.505)

Questioner: Why do parents become suspicious about us even when we have a platonic relationship with our male friends?

Dadashri: You can never have such a relationship with a boy. It is not possible. It is wrong to be friends with boys.

Questioner: What is wrong with that?

Dadashri: It would be like putting fire and fuel together. Together they will ignite! Both look for an opportunity to take advantage of the other. Each is like a hunter in search of prey.

Questioner: You have said that boys and girls should not have friendships with each other.

Dadashri: Yes, absolutely not.

Questioner: People will not accept this, Dada.

Dadashri: That may be so, but I have seen situations where such friendships have created terrible problems. The girls have become pregnant and committed suicide, while the boys have remained unaffected. (P.506)

When you reach a marriageable age, let your parents know that you are ready to get married and to find you a suitable boy who will stay with you throughout the rest of your life. Do not be bashful about it. Just tell them that Dada has told you to ask them. And within a couple of years you can get married after you both approve of each other. Men will no longer desire you once they know that you are spoken for.

It is not good to have boyfriends. They will ultimately take advantage of you. They can be very deceptive and untrustworthy and they will not think about your welfare.

Marriage is the best thing for you. You will not get anywhere if you keep wandering around. Your parents are settled and they no longer have any problems. You should also do the same. Does that not appeal to you? Would you rather roam around? Do you not understand my point? (P.509)

Girls ask me why I tell them to get married. I tell them that they should either get married or take a vow of celibacy. They must make a decision one way or another and stick to that decision firmly. When I ask them why they object to getting married, they tell me that boys nowadays have no personalities, so what is the use of marrying such imbeciles? Their boldness surprised me. They are so aggressive even before marriage that I thought to myself what will become of their poor husbands. Some of the boys too say that they would rather not get married. I tell the girls that they must get rid of this opinion of theirs because they have no alternative but get married. If they were to marry with the notion that boys are imbeciles, they will also see their husbands as such, and will always have problems in their marriage. (P.510)

This whole world is evolving towards liberation, but it is the

Generation Gap

clashes and conflicts amongst people that create obstacles along the way. It is the very nature of a hot scorching summer to pull after it a season of monsoon rains. As the summer heat intensifies, it will bring the rains. There is no need for one to be afraid of anything.

In the same way, the nature of the worldly life is that it will steer you towards liberation, pulling moksha towards you like a magnet. The harsher the worldly life becomes, the quicker the Soul's libration will come. One should not succumb to life's ruthlessness, but hold on to his position on the stage. Understand that adverse circumstances are a vitamin for the Soul and worldly happiness is a vitamin for the physical body. Go through life with this understanding. Everyday you are bound to get some vitamin for the Soul. From my very childhood, I have been enjoying both vitamins, whereas you only look for the vitamin for the body.

Have you not seen people fast and do all kinds of rigid penance for the sake of their Souls? To them, their penance is their Soul's vitamin. But you are fortunate to receive your vitamins for the Soul, in the comforts of your own home. (P. 522)

Do not set your heart on a love marriage. There are no guarantees as to what your partner's temperament will be like later on. When your parents find you a boy, you can look at him critically. Make sure he has reasonable intelligence and has no major defects. You should feel attraction towards him. You should be attracted to him.

Questioner : Can parents make a mistake in their choice of a boy for us?

Dadashri : Their intention is to do the best for you. Despite this, if something goes wrong, it is your destiny, that which you have brought with you from your past life. So what can anyone do then? The risks are greater when you look for a spouse on your own. Many marriages have failed in this way. (P. 525)

A mahatma's only son expressed to me his wish to get married. I asked him what sort of girl he wanted to marry and he said that he would do whatever I asked of him. He also added that his own mother was very shrewd when it came to choosing a wife for him, which meant that he had already accepted the idea of his mother picking his marriage partner for him. This is exactly how it should be. (P.527)

Questioner : My daughter is very opposed to the idea of an arranged marriage. She thinks that her life will be ruined and says that she would rather become acquainted with the boy and see him several times before consenting to marry him. What should I do about her?

Dadashri : They fight anyway despite getting to know one another prior to the marriage. The couples who accepted their arranged marriage and did not become acquainted with each other prior to their marriage, are doing very well, because they have accepted what nature has offered them, while in the other case they try to use their own intellect. (P.528)

A daughter of a mahatma refused to marry a well-educated boy her parents had painstakingly found for her and felt that he was ideal. They both liked him very much and when she refused to marry him, it upset them tremendously. In his frustration, the father came to me and I told him that I would speak to his daughter. I asked her why she did not like the boy, and whether it was because of his size or his height. She said that it was because his complexion was a little dark. I told her that if that was the only problem, she should go ahead and consent to him and that I would make him fair. She even confronted her father why he had come

Generation Gap

all the way to complain to me. What else could the poor man do? After she got married, one day I asked her whether she wanted me to order some special soap to make his complexion fair and she replied that it was not necessary and that he was already fair enough. There was no need for her to be so overly concerned about his complexion. I thought he was a fine boy. How could they let go of such a nice boy? (P.531)

Questioner : Is dating a sin? When girls and boys go out together, is it a sin? Is there anything wrong in it?

Dadashri : Yes. If you feel like going out with boys, then you should get married. You should decide on just one boy and stick to him. Until you get married you should not involve yourself with any boys.

Questioner : In America and England, when boys and girls turn fourteen years of age they begin dating. If they like someone they will continue dating each other and their relationship will progress. Sometimes after they have been dating for a long time, they will separate because something goes wrong or they stop liking each other. Then they will start dating someone else and if that does not workout, they will date someone else. Everything just moves around in circles, and sometimes they maybe dating more than two or three people at the same time

Dadashri : That is all wildness. That is a wild life.

Questioner : Then what should they do?

Dadashri : There should be sincerity and a commitment to just one person. Your life should be like this. A boy should be sincere to just one girl and vice versa. An insincere life is wrong.

Questioner : How can a person remain sincere if the other person changes and becomes insincere?

Dadashri: Then stop dating altogether. Get married. After all, we are humans, not uncivilized!

After marriage you should live sincerely with each other. If you want to live sincerely, then you should not be involved with any other man from the very beginning. You should be very strict in this matter. If you want to date someone, do so with the idea in your mind that you will marry him. Tell your parents that you have decided to marry him and no one else. An insincere life is a wild life. (P.532)

Would you tolerate it if a person had a bad reputation and had many addictions?

Questioner: Absolutely not.

Dadashri: And what if his character was good but he had an addiction?

Questioner: I would only tolerate it if that addiction were for cigarettes, nothing else.

Dadashri: You are right. Smoking is tolerable. Alcohol is not to be tolerated. You have said well. Good character is very important. Do you believe that?

Questioner: Of course! How can one live without it?

Dadashri: Yes, if Indian girls and women understood just this much, a lot would be accomplished. To understand the importance of character is enough.

Questioner: Our noble thinking has developed as a result of reading good literature.

Dadashri: Very good. I am pleased. (P. 536)

Deception and insincerity is rampant everywhere. You do

Generation Gap

not see this but I can see everything. Wherever there is insincerity, there can never be happiness. You should remain sincere. When you get married, you should accept whatever mistakes the other person had made prior to the marriage and after that both of you should remain sincere to each other. You should not look at anyone else after your marriage. Once you are married, you must remain sincere, whether you like it or not. Do you not remain sincere to your mother, even when you do not like her? Are you not sincere to her even when she has disagreeable traits? (P.540)

Questioner : I accept that everything happens according to my own karma. But how do I deal with an insincere husband with equanimity?

Dadashri : If your husband is insincere, how can you win him over? Whatever your fate has in store, it will not leave you alone. Things do not go according to our wishes in this world. Come to me and I will give you guidance and knowledge of how to deal with him.

In Aurangabad, a Muslim girl named Masroor came to our satsang. I asked her to come and sit next to me. She looked into my eyes and felt a sense of peace and decided to stay. She told me that she was a lecturer and her fiancé was a lawyer in Pakistan and that they were to be married in six months. I told her that at the moment she was happy, but what would she do if after getting married, her husband made her unhappy. Did she have some sort of a plan as to how she would handle such a situation? Surely she must have thought about how she would get along with her husband. She told me that she was prepared. If he were to say something to her, she would have a response for it. She said that she had a response for everything he could possibly say.

Just like Russia and USA, she had prepared for a cold

war! She had made preparations to tackle all disputes. She was ready to fire before he could even begin. If he fired a torpedo, she would fire back with an equally powerful weapon. I informed her that she had begun a cold war, for which there would be no end.

Girls have a tendency to act this way. These poor boys are naive, they do not plan for anything and consequently they lose the battle.

I asked Masroor who had taught her all this and told her that if she were to carry on in this way, her husband was bound to divorce her within the first six months and whether that was what she wanted. I told her that her approach was very wrong. She protested that if she did not act this way, he would become her oppressor. I reassured her and told her that she should listen to my advice if she wanted a happy marriage. I told her all the women who had prepared to fight back with their husbands had failed miserably. I explained to her that she should go without anticipating any antagonism from him and not make any preparations for conflicts. If she went on fighting with her husband day in and day out, would he not think about other women? She would only win him over with love.

Questioner : Love?

Dadashri : Yes, love. There is an element of love even in attachment. I told her that she did not hate him and it was not a war between India and Pakistan. Everyone in a marriage seems to be at war. This brings misery into their lives.

I explained to her that in order to win her husband over, if he created any conflicts, she should try to resolve them. She should remain calm and not lose her temper. Even if he tried to create differences between the two of them, she should act as though they both were one. All these relationships are relative relationships;

Generation Gap

they are temporary and if both the parties end up tearing things, the marriage would end up in a divorce.

Masroor asked me what she should do. I told her that she should act according to his moods. If he is in a bad mood, she should instead talk to the Lord within him, and when his mood changes, then she can talk to him directly. If he were to say something hurtful to her, she should remain silent. She should see him as innocent. He acts according to the forces of his past karmas; in reality he is not the doer. Love is tolerance and adjustments. Love should be true. Feeble love will last only a short while. I told her that under no circumstances should she retaliate. Instead she should just remember 'Dada' and pray to Him for strength.

Masroor accepted everything. I told her that she should deal with her mother-in-law in the same way. I explained to her what strength of character is: Whenever her husband yelled at her, if she remained silent and calmly observed what was happening, her character would strengthen and it would have an impact on her husband. He would be impressed at her ability to remain calm and collected. He would lose the battle.

She followed my advice and acted on it. When one prepares to win a battle, they lose their inner energies. I never prepare for any battles. You might feel that in demonstrating your strength you are winning, but in fact, you are really losing your inner energies and strength of character. If you lose this, your husband will not value you at all. She understood this well and promised that she would never fight with him.

If someone is preparing to fight with you, and if you get ready to retaliate, your strength of character will break. No matter how much someone tries to provoke you into a fight, if you do not respond to him, he will loose.

If you prepare to retaliate, you will be pulled into his trap. So many people have tried to thwart me but they have lost at their own game, because I never think about retaliation. When you even think about retaliation, you will lose your strength of character.

A shilvan person is someone who remains calm in all adversities. If someone tries to harm a shilvan, he would not be able to do so. The moment the aggressor sees his face; he would lose his nerve to do harm. Such is the impact of a shilvan. If you prepare to retaliate in any situation, you will lose your shil; your inner strength. Let others do whatever they wish. Such a person is one with every one else. (P.542)

When faced with conflicts, we are forced to prepare for our own defense. When we do this, we fall. Now, after this Gnan, we no longer have the ammunition to retaliate. The other person may have the weapon so let him use it. Everything is vyavasthit and that vyavasthit is such that his own weapon will hurt him.

Later Mashroor brought her own father, a doctor, for Dada's darshan. If a person has problems, all he has to do is come to me and his work will be done. (P.549)

All your problems can be solved. Each word of mine will carry a solution for your problems and take you all the way to moksha. So Adjust everywhere. (P.550)

HAPPINESS IN LIFE THROUGH SERVICE

Children who see faults in their parents will never be happy. They may have material wealth, but they would never be happy spiritually. You must never see faults in your parents. How can you forget what they have done for you? You do not forget someone's kindness even when they offer you a cold drink on a hot day, so how can you forget your parents' kindness?

Generation Gap

Care for them in the best possible way. If they say something disagreeable to you, overlook it. They are your elders. Do you think they deserve disrespect?

Questioner : No. But what if it happens by mistake?

Dadashri : Why do you not fall by mistake? You manage to be careful in that situation. Besides, if you slip accidentally, your father will understand, but if you make a mistake on purpose, he will question you. Try your best not to make a mistake. If it happens outside your control they will understand and know that you are not capable of doing it. Keep them happy. Do they not try to keep you happy? All parents desire their child's happiness.

(P.563)

Questioner : Yes, but I feel that they have got into a habit of nagging.

Dadashri : Yes, then it is your own fault and you have to do pratikraman for hurting them. They should not be hurt. You should tell yourself that you are here to keep them happy. Ask yourself what you did to make them unhappy. (P.564)

Do you think your father is bad? What will happen when you think badly of him? There is nothing bad in this world. Whatever comes your way is precise and it is justice. A mother is a mother and you should never see any faults in her. Destiny has given her to you. Can you ever replace your mother?

Questioner : No.

Dadashri : Can you purchase a mother? Even if you could, she would be no good to you. What good is a fair and pretty mom? The mother that you have is good and she is the one for you. You should not compare her with someone else's mother. You should praise her for what she is.

Questioner : What should we feel about our father?

Dadashri : Keep him happy. (P.564)

Parents are parents. Your primary obligation in this world is your duty to your parents. Will you take care of them?

Questioner : Yes, I help around the house. (P. 565)

Dadashri : Do you want peace?

Questioner : Yes. I do.

Dadashri : I will help you with that, but have you ever taken care of your parents? You will always have peace if you take care of them. Nowadays, people do not help and they do not take care of their parents sincerely. At the age of thirty, the boy finds a guru (wife) who demands to be taken to a new home. Have you seen such a guru? After the age of twenty or thirty years he changes because of his guru. When she complains about his mother, at first he refuses to listen but eventually he agrees with her and begins to resent his own mother.

People, who wholeheartedly care for their parents, find peace. That is the law of nature. People ask me what fault lies on their part, when their children do not care for them. I tell them it is because the parents themselves never cared for their own parents. This entire generation has gone astray. If a new one began all over, it would be a better one. (P.566)

This science of the Soul flourishes by caring for the elderly. People revere and worship stone idols and look after them, but do the idols have aching limbs or feelings? The elderly, the parents and the guru should be served and cared for. (P.567)

Your duty and religion is to care for your parents. Regardless of the kind of karmic accounts you have with them, they should be cared for. You will receive as much happiness as you give to them.

I ran into a man at an ashram. He told me that he had been living there for the last ten years. I knew his parents and told him that they were poverty-stricken, suffering tremendously and dying. He told me that he was helpless and could not do anything for them because if he were to leave the ashram to take care of them, he would be neglecting his religious practices. How can anyone call this religion? Religion is to care for others. People's worldly interactions should be ideal. How can any interaction that causes a person to neglect his own parents be considered religion?

(P.569)

In the prime of my youth I took good care of my mother. I was able to do at least that much. For my father, all I managed to do was carry his body over my shoulders at his funeral. I realized later on that such was my karmic account and that I must have had countless fathers like him in my previous lives. What more could I do then? I found the answer and it was to take care of the elders that were living. Those who have departed are gone forever. Take care of the ones who are living. It is better to start now, although late, than never. It is a great blessing to take care of the living parents. The rewards are immediate. They are next to God; although you cannot see God, you can see them. (P.570)

It is the elderly that suffer the most, but to whom can they complain? Their children do not pay any attention to them. The generation gap is too wide between the old and the new. The old people cannot change and adjust to the new pace of life, even if they suffer.

Questioner : Every old person is in the same situation.

Dadashri : Yes it is the same everywhere. What can be

done to address this problem? It would be wonderful if there were special living arrangements for the elderly. First and foremost, they should be given this Gnan. After that various public and social services can handle their daily meals and requirements. But Gnan is of utmost importance because it will give them peace and further their spiritual progress. There is no way for them to find peace otherwise. What do you think? (P.570)

What kind of moral values do your children learn at home? When you bow down to your parents, even at your age, will it not encourage your children to do the same? Would the children then not do the same to you? (P.573)

Questioner : Children today do not bow down to their parents. They seem reluctant or ashamed to do so.

Dadashri : They do not because they do not revere their parents. Too often they see the parents fighting and they see a lot of negative interactions between them, which is why they do not respect their parents. If they perceive good thoughts and see good conduct in their parents, they would bow down to their parents all the time. But today parents fight in front of their children, do they not?

Questioner : Yes.

Dadashri : So how can the parents expect their children to respect them? (P.574)

In this world you must have the highest reverence towards your father, your mother and your guru. You cannot forget the benevolence of those who have guided you to the right path.

(P.575)

JAI SAT CHIT ANAND

GLOSSARY

Atma	The Self or Soul, also denotes the Supreme Soul or Paramatma
Acharyas	Preceptors
Agnas	Principles; instructions
Ahankar	Ego
Akram	Without a specific method or step or order
Alochana	Recall of agression
Anhak	That which does not belong to you.
Antaraya karma	Obstructing karma
Atma Dharma	Religion of the Self
Atma Gnan	Knowledge of the Selef
Avaran	Veil, covering
Avatar	Life time
Avlamban	Support
Avtar	Life form
Bhaav	Intention
Bhagwan	God
Bhakti	Reverence, devotionalism, worship.
Buddhi	Intellect
Chandubhai	Name of the worldy being.
Charan Vidhi	Booklet to be read following Gnan Vidhi
Charitrabud	Power behind good
Chit	The component within which sees that which has been known. It is like a photograph of an actual event.
Dada	Gnani Purush Ambalal Patel
Dada Bhagwan	The fully enlightened Self
Darshan	To view, see

Dharma	Duty, Attribute
Dharmada	Good deeds for others
Dowry	Properties and money brought by a wife at marriage
Dwesh	Aversion, Abhorrence
Farajiyat	Duty bound; obligatory duty
Ghee	Refined butter
Gita	The religious scripture of Hindu religion.
Gnan	Knowledge, knowledge of the Self.
Gnani Purush	One who has realized the Self and is the instrument for the salvation of the world.
Guru	Teacher, master
Hiraba	Dada's wife
Hisaab	Account of karma
Jagruti	Awareness
Jain	One who studies the science of the Enlightened.
Jiva	Living things
Kaliyug	Era of despair, the current time cycle also known as doosham kaal, characterized by a progressive decline in spiritual knowledge and consequently, the degeneration of human civilization
Karma	Deeds or actions that covers the Soul and prevents liberation.
Khichdi	A simple rice and lentil dish
Khuda	God
Kramik	Step by step
Ksatriyas	Member of warrior cast

Lakh	100,000
Laxmi	Goddess of wealth and prosperity
Lord Mahavir	The twenty fourth Tirthankara, the last of the 24 of the descending half of the current time cycle.
Maan	Respect, false pride
Magas	A sweet
Marajiyat	According to your own will, freewill
Moha	Infatuation, attachment.
Moksha	Liberation of Soul from karmas, from the cycle of birth and death.
Narak	Hellish life; hell; the world of infernal beings
Niralamb	Without dependance on anything
Nirjiva	Non-living;
Parmanus	Atoms; smallest particle of matter
Paramatma	God; the Supreme Self; fully realized Self.
Prakriti	Nature
Prarabdha	Destiny; in course of fruition.
Pratikraman	Apology coupled with remorse for any wrongdoing; reversal of aggression.
Pratyakhan	Resolution never to repeat the mistake again
Pudgal	The relative self; matter, that which fills and empties.
Punya	Merit karma
Raag	Attachment
Rakshash	Demon
Rupees	Indian currency
Sadhus	Sage; monk devoted to Self-realization

Sambhav	Equanimity; to remain undisturbed
Sambhave nikal	To settle with equanimity
Sansar	Worldly life; mundane affairs; cycle of birth and death
Sanskar	Moral value; innate tendencies, value system.
Satsang	The company of the Self. That which leads to the company of the Self.
Sheth	A rich man
Shilvan	One with the highest qualities
Shuddhatma	Pure Soul
Sukh	Happiness
Surya Narayan	Sun God
Talaak	Divorce in Islam.
Tiryanch Gati	Migration of self into non-humans like birds, animals, insects, plants etc.
Vaishnav	A devotee of Lord Vishnu or Krishna; faith of such person.
Vignan	Science
Vyavahar	Social relations; worldly affairs through thought, speech and action.

❖❖❖❖❖

Books of Akram Vignan of Dada Bhagwan
1. Adjust Everywhere
2. Ahimsa : Non-Violence
3. Anger
4. Aptavani 1
5. Aptavani 2
6. Aptavani 6
7. Aptavani 9
8. Autobiography of Gnani Purush A.M.Patel
9. Avoid Clashes
10. Brahmacharya : Celibacy Attained With Understanding
11. Death : Before, During & After...
12. Flawless Vision
13. Generation Gap
14. Harmony In Marriage
15. Life Without Conflict
16. Money
17. Noble Use of Money
18. Pratikraman : The master key that resolves all conflicts
19. Pure Love
20. Right Understanding to Help Others
21. Science of Karma
22. Science of Speech
23. Shree Simandhar Swami : The Living God
24. The Essence Of All Religion
25. The Fault Is Of the Sufferer
26. The Guru and The Disciple
27. Tri Mantra : The mantra that removes all worldly obstacles
28. Whatever Happened is Justice
29. Who Am I ?
30. Worries

'Dadavani' Magazine is published Every month

Persons to Contact

Dada Bhagwan Parivar

Adalaj : **Trimandir**, Simandhar City, Ahmedabad-Kalol Highway, Adalaj, Dist.: Gandhinagar - 382421, Gujarat, India.
Tel : (079) 39830100, Email : info@dadabhagwan.org

Ahmedabad : **"Dada Darshan"**, 5, Mamtapark Society, B/h. Navgujarat College, Usmanpura, Ahmedabad- 380 014.
Tel. : (079) 27540408, 27543979

Rajkot : **Trimandir**, Ahmedabad-Rajkot Highway, Nr. Targhadiya Cross Road, Maliyasan Village, Rajkot. Tel.: 9274111393

Vadodara : **"Dada Mandir"**, 17, Mama ni pol (Dada Bhagwan Street), Opp. Raopura Police Station, Salatvada, Vadodara.
Tel. : (0265) 2414142, 9825032901

Other than Gujarat :

Mumbai : Dada Bhagwan Parivar, Mobile : 9323528901-03
Kolkata : Dada Bhagwan Parivar, Mobile : 9330333885
Bangalore : Dada Bhagwan Parivar, Mobile : 9341948509

U.S.A. : **Dada Bhagwan Vignan Institute** : Dr. Bachu Amin, 100, SW Redbud Lane, Topeka, Kansas 66606
Tel : +1 785 271 0869, Email : bamin@cox.net
Dr. Shirish Patel, 2659, Raven Circle, Corona, CA 92882
Tel.:+1 951 734 4715, Email:shirishpatel@sbcglobal.net

U.K. : **Dada Centre**, 236, Kingsbury Road, (Above Kingsbury Printers), Kingsbury, London, NW9 0BH
Tel. : +44 07956 476253
Email : dadabhagwan_uk@yahoo.com

Canada : **Dinesh Patel**, 4, Halesia Drive, Etobicock, Toronto, M9W 6B7. **Tel.** : +1 416 675 3543
E-mail: ashadinsha@yahoo.ca

Australia : +61-2-96385702; **Dubai** : +971 506754832
Singapore : +65 81129229

Website : www.dadabhagwan.org & www.dadashri.org